The Greatest Book Ever Written About Cheese

By
LEN ROBBINS

Indigo Custom Publishing, LLC

Publisher	Henry S. Beers
Associate Publisher	Richard J. Hutto
Executive Vice President	Robert G. Aldrich
Operations Manager	Gary G. Pulliam
Editor-in-Chief	Joni Woolf
Art Director/Designer	Julianne Gleaton
Designer	Daniel Emerson
Director of Marketing and Public Relations	Mary D. Robinson

Printed in U.S.A.

Library of Congress Control Nmber: 2006935839

ISBN: (10 Digit) 1-934144-05-3   ISBN: (13 Digit) 978-1-934144-05-3

Indigo Custom Publishing, LLC books are available at quantity discounts with bulk purchase for educational, business, or sales promotional use.

For information, please write to:
Indigo Custom Publishing, LLC • SunTrust Bank Building • 435 Second St. • Suite 320 • Macon, GA 31201, or call toll free 866-311-9578.

This book is dedicated in memory of my grandmother,

Mrs. Ann Robbins

I miss you.

TABLE OF CONTENTS

PREFACE

The compliment was of the left-handed variety.

"Hey, why don't you put all your best columns in a book? I'd buy it," an unknown caller told me years ago.

"Well, thanks," I responded warmly. "I'll consider that."

"Yeah, see, that way, I won't have to buy a paper when you write a stupid one," he added, extinguishing my moment of glee.

Since that time, I've heard the same request numerous times – or something akin – about compiling my newspaper columns in book form for public consumption.

Admittedly, the majority of those suggestions came from my mother, but there were others as well, mostly from readers in prison (where I enjoy odd, immense popularity).

And thus, I present "The Greatest Book Ever Written About Cheese." Why "The Greatest Book Ever Written About Cheese"? Well, first off, "The Adventures of Huckleberry Finn" was already taken.

A more detailed explanation of the reasoning behind the title can be found on Page 65 of this tome (entitled "Scantily-clad Mandrell Sisters write book about candy"). You'll have to read it to understand, although that may not actually help either.

Another reason this book is titled "The Greatest Book Ever Written About Cheese" is that we are trying to penetrate a market heretofore ignored by the book publishing industry – cheese-eaters who read. The way I figure it: People who eat cheese + people who read = People who would buy "The Greatest Book Ever Written About Cheese."

Yes, I realize I am very clever.

I wanted to categorize these columns in alphabetical order by height, but was swayed to settle for chronological order after it was explained to me what that meant.

The first column in this book was written back in 1997, when I was freshly married to my beautiful bride. The last entry is from May of 2006, where I comment in detail about the trials of being the father of three.

Following the columns from front to back, you will basically see a mini-autobiographical succession (notice I didn't say maturation) of my life, from my days as a childless newlywed through the birth of our first child, then second, then third, and all the wild and wonderful wackiness in between.

I appreciate my family (who shall remain nameless to protect them from humiliation/celebrity), and especially my wife, for allowing me to share our tales of woe, pity, woe, despair, and pitiful woe. I don't know what I'm going to do when our youngest child learns to read and realizes how he's been used all these years. The gig will be up. There's always barber college, I guess.

In addition to my wife, who's a great sport and kind critic, I'd also like to take this opportunity to thank all of my friends in the newspaper community who have been so kind as to carry my columns in their newspapers. Particularly, I'd like to thank Bo McLeod of *The Donalsonville News*, Kim Madlom, formerly of *The Thomaston Times,* and Tim Anderson of the *Herald-Leader* in Fitzgerald – who were among the first newspaper folks to take a chance on this newly-minted syndicated columnist. I'm also greatly indebted to Robert and Cheryl Williams of *The Blackshear Times*, who are cherished mentors and friends.

Lastly, I would like to thank my new friends at Indigo Publishing and Henchard Press for being so gullible as to fall for publishing this.

So, to the gentlemen caller and his sorted brethren, here's the book you wanted. You be the judge if I left in a "stupid one." (I did).

Len Robbins
October 2, 2006

The greatest column ever written about cheese

From February 26, 1997

My name is Len Robbins, and I love cheese.

I love cheese of all kinds – from cheddar to Swiss to Cheez-its to reruns of "Chips." It nourishes my tummy, warms my innards, and makes me happy on sad, rainy days.

Through the years, cheese has undergone many manifestations, from its early days as a car polish to its current usages in products such as cheese-flavored corn puffs and Cheese-On-A-Stick.

In this space, I'd like to take a closer look at cheese – its past, its present, and its magnificent effect on mankind. Let's take a gander.

Cheese Through the Ages: Just when the first cheese was first manufactured is not known, but its existence is recorded as early as 8000 B.C. According to legend, cheese was first made by wandering Asiatic tribes who, when looking for a hamburger topping, discovered that a curd prepared from milk made a tasty treat. Then called "stuff that comes from curd," the food was later named in honor of a nomadic, large-headed mouse, Chuck E. Cheese.

In its infant stages, cheese was used for practical as well as nutritional purposes. Ancient scribes say Moses used the product as a type of makeshift glue for a chipped tablet portion of the Ten Commandments. In early 13th-century France, baked cheese made for a snappy chapeau. And, a couple of years later, our country's first president, George Washington, used cheese to grip his dentures into place.

Cheese oddities: There are many types of edible cheese, but one of the most puzzling is Limburger.

Many of you may remember Limburger as the cheese with the putrid odor that was used as the protagonist for many practical jokes by the "Little Rascals" on their television program.

Limburger was first developed as an insect repellent in 1793 by Belgian physicist Hans Limburger (known in Belgium as "the George Washington Carver of Cheese"). Since then, scientists and Stymie alike have been baffled as to why someone – no one knows exactly who – one day said, "this is the foulest, most disgusting thing I have ever smelled. I think I'll eat it."

With the success of Limburger cheese at grocery stores as an edible product, other efforts to market stinky cheese products quickly fell into line. But despite massive sales campaigns, "Kraft Funky Cheese," and "Nabisco's Reeking Cheese Chips" never found an audience.

The Decline of Cheese: In the late 1970s, the sour cream and onion lobby successfully sullied cheese's good name with a smear campaign – alleging that cheese was fattening and unhealthy.

The creation of such products as fried cheese, dubbed the "The World's Most Fattening (and Yummy) Food" have done little to improve cheese's damaged image.

Cheese Fights Back: Cheese has made something of a comeback in recent years. Breakthroughs in scientific technology have brought us wonderful products like fat-free cheese, healthy cheese substitutes, and Cheez-Whiz – all bringing cheese back into the hearts, and stomachs, of eaters everywhere.

Blessed are the cheesemakers. And cheese-eaters too.

Selective hearing wins new convert
April 30, 1997

Some of my fellow Clinch Countians may remember that we had two foreign exchange students visit us back in the mid-1980s.

One of them was a young Brazilian man named Alvaro, who was from Sao Paolo, Brazil, which is known as the "New York City" of Brazil, although it's called Sao Paolo (pronounced ja-ja-a-'ran-shee).

With his cosmopolitan background, Alvaro was a little more sophisticated than his newfound countrified comrades, who were in awe when he told us that in some places in Sao Paolo, people actually park your car for you. Needless to say, we were flabbergasted.

And while we yokels were supposed to be teaching Alvaro about America, he ended up teaching us something things which I carry to this day.

For instance, Alvaro taught me a little trick I call selective hearing. He called it something else I didn't understand.

Alvaro was very smart, and could speak and understand English remarkably well – when he wanted to.

When he didn't want to – well, he didn't.

"Alvaro, do you have your homework?"

Suddenly, the suave multilinguist became a Portuguese dock worker.

"Me no understand English," he would say.

The teacher would then raise her voice, as if deafness was his problem.

"Do... you... have... your... homework?"

Alvaro would look at her, confused. "Me eat sandwich for lunch – Yes."

She would then grab another student's homework. "See this, Alvaro. Do... you... have... this, your... homework?"

Alvaro would then grab a piece of paper off his desk. "Yes, pencil. Me write with pencil."

Frustrated, the teacher would start again and then tail off in mid-sentence. "Do... you... oh, never mind."

Minutes later, Alvaro was out in the hall, reciting the Declaration of Independence.

And while Alvaro's mode of selective hearing was more associated with understanding language, I have taken his little scam and crafted it to fit my own needs.

"Honey, will you come help me retile this bathroom floor," my wife will call to me as I relax on the couch, embroiled in SportsCenter.

"Huh?"

This time, louder. "Will you come help me retile this bathroom floor?!"

"What?"

Even louder. "Will you come and help me retile this floor in the bathroom?!"

"Huh?"

Now screaming – "Will... you... oh, never mind."

Yes, love is the international language – if you feel like hearing it.

Today's youth should be thankful for remote control

March 4, 1998

I'm not much for paying attention, but a small detail in a movie I was watching the other night caught my eye and peaked my very limited interest.

The movie was "That Thing You Do," which is about the rise and fall of a pop band in the 1960s. In the film, one scene shows an excited family watching their son, who is the band's drummer, on television performing. During this scene, the father tells the wife "to hand him the remote control."

This struck me as odd, which later led to confusion, then anger, then I forgot all about it and ate some Funyuns.

The problem I had with this scene, and particularly the inclusion of the remote control, is that I believed television remote controls to be a product of the late 1970s at the earliest.

If remote controls were around since the 1960s, as the film contends, then two generations of Americans, and some Canadians, have been bamboozled, and the meaning of life has lost a bit of its luster.

For instance, when I was growing up, in the 1970s and early 1980s, remote controls were non-existent. Only families that gave their kids ponies for their birthdays could afford remote control devices.

During those days, children were remote controls.

I remember vividly standing next to the television set every night, changing channels for my father.

"Turn it to Channel Four," he would say, catching a glimpse of "That's My Mama." "Okay, turn it to Channel Two... okay, Channel 10... alright, Channel Four."

This would go on every night for a couple of hours, and produced a generation of strong-legged, nimble-fingered youth.

"What'd you do last night?"

"Changed channels," my fellow fourth-graders would answer.

"Yeah, me too," I would respond, privately wondering how my father could possibly enjoy both "Hee Haw" and "Sanford and Son" equally.

I'm sure this was one of those type of things handed down from generation to generation. I imagine my father grew up changing channels for his father back in the 1950s, and I followed the rite of passage.

5

In fact, it is now accepted by a limited few that most children from 1945-1982 were created for the sole purpose of being remote controls.

While the popularly-held theory is that the Baby Boomer generation came about in relation to the end of World War II, myself, scientists, sociologists, and bus drivers have developed an alternative reason for the increase in births during that period – the advent of television.

With more television sets came a bigger need for remote controls, i.e., children, and hence, people started reproducing like mad. The next generation followed suit.

Then, remote controls entered the mainstream, signalling the end of this cycle, and the beginning of blissful laziness everywhere, a reduction in the birth rate, and an increase in lily-legged, stubby-fingered children.

Remote controls in the 1960s? Considering the evidence against it, I don't think so.

A man's search for another man named Daryl

June 24, 1998

I was in my office, after hours, when the call came. I happened to be on the other line.

"Hello, Clinch County News," I said, putting a friend on hold. Seconds passed. No response. I tried again. "Hello?"

I waited a few more seconds. My finger was on the button to switch back to the other call when I heard a low, guttural voice.

"Daryl?"

"No, this is the Clinch County News," I said.

"Huh?"

I waited for a few more seconds, figuring the person on the other line would realize they had the wrong number. No dice.

"Daryl, is that you?"

"No, there is no Daryl here. You've reached the Clinch County News."

"Is Daryl there?"

"No, there's no Daryl here," I said calmly.

"Who's this?"

"This is Len Robbins," I replied.

"Who?" His tone implied that I shouldn't be there, or that maybe I should be Daryl, which I thought about becoming.

"There's no Daryl here. I've got another call," I said, trying to give a hint.

"Do you know Daryl's number?"

"No, I don't."

My reply apparently confused him, for a few seconds lapsed before his monotone emerged refreshed, this time perky with inspiration.

"Hey, can you look up Daryl's number for me?"

"No, maybe you need to look in the book," I said, my patience still intact. "I've got another call, and..."

"What book?"

"The phone book," I said. The mere mention of a book stymied my phone pal's thought process.

A few more moments passed.

"Do you know where Daryl's at?"

"No, I don't know where Daryl's at." Again, a lapse of silence while his wheels turned oh-so-slowly.

"Do you got Daryl's number?"

"No, I'm sorry," I said, exasperated. "I don't have Daryl's number." This time, his tone turned.

"Well, then, thanks for nothing," he bellowed. "I'll just call 911."

Somewhere, there's a man who is probably licensed to drive a car, looking for another man named Daryl.

Scary.

Respect football season's ill victims, please
September 2, 1998

To many men in the South, the worldwide-accepted seasons of Spring, Summer, Fall, and Winter do not exist.

In their world, there are two seasons of the year: Football season and Football Recruiting season (also throw in Hunting season for some).

The months between March and August don't really matter to these folks. Those are, of course, the hibernation months.

This seasonal variance is not by choice. Like other uncontrollable illnesses, such as not being able to wash dishes or not being able to put down the toilet seat, it's caused by a mutant gene that some men are born with. Science has found no cure, nor are they looking for one.

It's just something these poor men have to cope with one day at a time.

With the football season now upon us, I have, in the interest of relationships everywhere, compiled a list of tips to help these men's seasonal illness be less painful.

In the sake of kindness, if you know a man that suffers from this ailment, follow these simple rules and wait for March:

• If he is in the backyard and the television in the den is on, that doesn't mean he's not watching it.

• Commercial breaks were made for a purpose.

They are the perfect time to ask questions, say what you need to say, or fetch your man a cold beverage.

• ESPN has a program called *SportsCenter* that comes on periodically throughout the day. It's sort of like church – not to be interrupted unless the house, or his clothes, are on fire (shoes don't count).

• A hot dog and a Coke at a ballgame does, in fact, constitute going out to dinner.

• At no time during football season should anyone have to take any type of Cosmo quiz unless the words "gridiron" and "Herschel" are both used.

• Dining etiquette is barred during football season.

• As decided by the 1979 U.S. Supreme Court ruling, *Men of the World vs. Mrs. Johnson,* furniture is not be moved at any time during football season.

Sorry, it's the law.

• Remember: The way you wear a hat does affect the way a team plays football.

• By all means, do not misplace the remote control. This causes hallucinations and uncontrollable drooling in some subjects.

• Lawn mowing on Wednesday night at 10:30 p.m. is perfectly acceptable during football season.

• When planning an event during the months of August-February, consult Athlon's Football Guide to determine if there are any football contests that day. Also, don't assume that your man is not interested in the Bowling Green-Akron game.

He is.

Learning responsibility the cold-fashioned way

September 9, 1998

It was exactly what I wanted.

Even though it was July and 101 degrees out, for my birthday, I had asked for a genuine NFL Atlanta Falcons letterman-type jacket out of the J.C. Penney's catalog, which I think cost around $35 - a bundle back in the mid '70s.

And on my birthday, I ripped through the wrapping like mad and there it was – just what I wanted. It was red with white leather sleeves. My parents, who had given me the jacket, issued two missives: Don't wear it until it gets cold; and take care of it. You won't get another one.

Apparently, I had already established somewhat of a reputation for losing things. I promised I would follow their rules, then proceeded to wear it around the house all summer, sweating profusely through July and August.

When the thermometer hit 72 degrees in mid-September, I unveiled the jacket before all my jealous elementary-school brethren.

"Just like the one Billy Ryckman wears," I told them, oblivious to the fact that I was the only one in my school who knew that Billy Ryckman was a little-used Falcon receiver.

Later in the school day, once the oohs and aahs had ceased for my new torso-wear, recess came. Not wanting to be bulked down while running around wildly, I placed my pride and joy in the jacket pile with the other clothing.

Forty-five minutes later, I returned to the jacket pile. Then panic struck. I searched once. I searched twice. I scanned the playground. I went to the main office to ask them if someone had turned in a genuine NFL Atlanta Falcons jacket. I called the president. No dice.

My jacket was gone, stolen by some pre-teen thief, now undoubtedly burning in eternity with Belzebub.

I didn't lift my head the rest of the day. When I got home, and my brand-new jacket wasn't with its proud owner, my parents alertly asked about the whereabouts of my birthday present. Too distraught to come up with a good lie, I told them my story of woe.

"Well, that was your jacket," my mother said. "And you said you would take care of it. Now, you're going to have to go all winter without a heavy jacket."

In my mind, that was unfair. I expected them to buy me another brand-new, genuine NFL Atlanta Falcons letterman jacket. Other parents would, I reasoned.

They would break, I thought, when I started shivering uncontrollably when the temperature dipped down to 40.

But they didn't. They bundled me up in a windbreaker and sent me to the bus stop, while all the other kids were wrapped in what amounted to blankets with sleeves. For three months, while the winter raged against my veil-thin windbreaker, my bus-stop comrades waited comfortably, calmly discussing the niceties of the day.

As my teeth chattered tunes I couldn't control, I had no idea I was learning a valuable lesson.

Others, the kids whose parents bought them a new jacket when they lost one, learned that lesson much later – usually with more severe consequences.

They call it "tough love" now. I called it freezing. But it worked for one.

The NBA has problems – I'm the answer

November 18, 1998

As you probably aren't aware, the National Basketball Association is currently in the midst of a holdout, with pro basketball players striking to improve their Gulag-like working conditions.

Their demands include a minimum salary of $1 million a year for all veteran players (no kidding) and all the dope they can smoke (kidding).

The NBA needs some new blood. Although my blood is old, I believe I am the answer to the NBA's woes. With that in mind, I have sent the following letter to NBA Commissioner David Stern.

Dear Mr. Stern:

First, I want to say that your new beard makes you look 20 years younger. I saw you on TV the other day and thought you were your son (if you have one. If you don't, you just look like some short, very handsome, young guy).

Anyway, I heard about the NBA players striking and wanted to officially volunteer my services to your league. Being a "scab" player does not scare me. I do not fear the real NBA players holding me in contempt. They already hold me in contempt because I make under $100,000 annually and I haven't fathered any illegitimate children.

I'm going to be honest with you. I'm the greatest basketball player that ever lived.

Well, actually, that's a lie. But I think that my unique combination of limited basketball skills, limited physical skills and unlimited charisma is exactly what you're looking for to put the "sket" back into basketball.

Consider my hoops accomplishments:

• I hold the all-time record at my high school for free throw percentage (100 percent) on the junior varsity, set during my sophomore year (2 of 2).

• I led the entire church league in assists per game (2.0) before being unfairly banned for life from the league for "excessive cursing."

• During my legendary high school career, I averaged 0.04 points per game, with a career high of four points (which I matched three times).

- During my senior year, I was carried off the court by crazed fans after hitting a 6-foot buzzer-beater to clinch an 85-44 victory.
- I once hit 11-of-25 free throws in practice.

I'm not the type of player you can stereotype as a "pure shooter" or a "playmaker" or a "rebounding machine" or "good." I defy stereotypes.

I'm not that strong a shooter, although I am deadly from two to three feet away from the basket when uncontested and nobody's talking. I've never considered myself fast, but a former coach once said that I was "as slow as a caveman." I have no idea what that means, but I'm going to assume that cavemen were extremely quick (having to run from dinosaurs and all).

I'm not much for defense. I find it tiring. On occasion, though, I have been known to steal a pass when it hits me directly in the chest area.

I am a ball-handling wizard, recently mastering the between-the-legs dribble after numerous hospitalizations.

In terms of rebounding, I try to avoid it.

I am 5'9" and not in particularly good shape, although I hustle like a madman when not gasping for air.

What I may lack in shooting ability, speed, defensive effort, ballhandling, rebounding skills, and physical prowess, I make up for with loads and loads of court savvy. My specialty is taking charges and diving recklessly for loose balls.

Simply put, I will be a fan favorite.

With that Michael Jordan guy long gone, I am prepared to take the reins as the NBA's marque player in terms of stellar, crowd-pleasing play, marketing opportunities and goofy antics.

Best of all, I won't take any pay for being your newest NBA superstar. No, unlike my greedy hoops brethren, I will play for free, only asking that all my expenses are paid for, unlimited Fritos, and the adulation of millions.

Hugs & kisses,
Len Robbins

P.S. If you could, Mr. Stern, please place me on your Harlem Globetrotters team. I've been working on my behind-the-back pass (a crowd favorite) and I think that Curly Neal and I would make a doozy of a backcourt tandem.

Life, patience, wallet drained by tire curse
From March 17, 1999

"...if it weren't for bad luck, I'd have no luck at all..."
– from "Hee Haw"

Luck doesn't travel with the Robbins clan.

Not that luck stays home much either, but it seems like every time we cross the Clinch County line on any type of journey, we are besieged with gloom, despair, and agony on us.

Our lucklessness usually manifests itself through, of all things, tires. This starts the chain effect that has come to be known as "The Great Life-Sucking, Patience-Testing, Wallet-Draining Cycle."

Since my wife and I have been married – three years – this cycle has occurred nearly a dozen times. The cycle includes a tire from one of our vehicles going flat. We have had brand-new tires go flat. We have had old, may-pop tires bust. The condition of the tire doesn't matter.

The flat tire always occurs on a Sunday, always when we are far away from home, always is discovered as we are preparing to leave, always requires us to search frantically for a place to plug or replace the tire when most everything is closed, and always, always prompts some type of financial hardship.

We aren't superstitious people. We don't believe in witches or warlocks or 24-hour dry cleaning. Only one of us has been abducted by a UFO. But the reasons for the flat tires has caused us to believe that someone, possibly the phone company, has placed a voodoo curse on us.

The following listing of our flat-tire mishaps is our evidence:

• 3/12/99 – Culprit: A roller skate.

While in Albany visiting family this past weekend, my wife runs over a roller skate hidden in leaves on a dirt road. The wheels had been taken off the roller skate, leaving jagged edges perfect for puncturing unsuspecting tires owned by Robbins family members.

• 10/11/98 – Culprit: A three-inch bolt.

Attending a wedding in Atlanta, we wake up to leave to find a flat tire. Further inspection reveals a three-inch bolt, mysteriously placed in our tire as we slept.

Four hours later, we leave Atlanta.

- 8/16/98 – Culprit: A chicken bone.

Again, after attending a wedding in Atlanta, we wake up to find a flat tire. Upon investigation at a gas station we had come to know well (read on), we find that a chicken bone had somehow infiltrated my wife's car tire, thus proving the curse angle (it's common knowledge that voodoo practitioners often use chicken bones, old Tab cans, and/or discarded refrigerator boxes in spell-casting).

- 6/14/98 – Culprit: A jumbo-sized toenail clipper.

In Atlanta shopping, we wake up Sunday morning... well, you know. We go to a gas station open on Sunday (the only one in the metro Atlanta area), which we would later revisit.

The gas station attendant is stunned that, somehow, a toenail clipper has flattened our tire.

- 4/12/98 – Culprit: A wrench.

This time, I was alone, near Patterson, Ga. A stranger pulled over to help me, and God bless him, somehow found a person to plug the tire. When he found a wrench with rounded edges inside my tire, he proclaimed that missing the race that Sunday afternoon was worth it.

- 11/5/97 – Culprit: A screwdriver.

This happened on my wife's birthday, in Atlanta. The previous night, while attending a wedding reception, I had locked the keys in the car, and we spent six hours trying to find someone to unlock her car door in Monroe, Ga., on a cold, cold Saturday night.

The screwdriver we found Sunday morning in my wife's tire was the first of the more popular tools to visit our tires. And made us both very happy.

I won't dabble into 1996 – the Year of the Nail – but you get the picture.

So, to whomever placed this curse on us, you'll be glad to know we've sworn off out-of-town trips for the next year. Hope you find that satisfactory.

The greatest pyramid scheme is inverted
March 31, 1999

A long time ago, at a newspaper far, far away, an editor got mad.

"Call Neal Inverted into my office!," the editor screamed out into the newsroom from his office.

Soon, young reporter Neal Inverted meekly walked into his seething editor's office.

"Neal, I want you to rewrite this story on how this lame-brained scientist thinks smoking is bad for you," the editor snarled while puffing on his stogie. "And I want you to put the important part first! I really don't care that this guy is from Cleveland, enjoys ballroom dancing, and has an ongoing feud with his distant cousin, President Chester A. Arthur. The most important part of the story is his harebrained notion that smoking isn't good for your health."

The deflated reporter wandered back to his typewriter and led his story with the scientist's outrageous claim.

Thus was born what has come to be known in journalism circles as the Inverted Pyramid style of writing news stories.

With the Inverted Pyramid, you get to the point from the get-go, then fill in the details in order of their relevance. This way, if the reader stops reading halfway through the story, they still get the gist of what the story is about.

Some of us newspaper folk are so ingrained into the Inverted Pyramid form of thinking that we expect it in all forms of communication.

"Hello, Mr. Robbins, I'm from the MCI," the cheery voice on the phone chirped. "How are you doing today?"

The Inverted Pyramid immediately kicks in.

"What are you selling?"

See, that saved about 10 minutes I would have never gotten back.

But some people just don't want a straightforward Inverted Pyramid society, where the wasted time used for superfluous jibber-jabber could be better utilized for the more important things in life – like eradicating world hunger, saving the rainforests, or building high-rise condos where jungles used to be.

My wife, for one, lives by the rule of Inverted Pyramid's evil nemesis – the Roundabout Circle.

"Len, I have something very important to ask you," she begins. I stop trying to eradicate hunger and listen up. "Caroline and I were talking yesterday about her living room. Do you remember how she decorated her living room, with the elongated mauve wall sconces?" I nod noncommittally, not understanding what she's talking about. "Well, I was watching Home & Garden yesterday and this woman had purchased something like that, but they were black and they matched the couches in her living room. Her living room looked like my cousin's. Remember, we went to their house a couple of years ago. She has that wonderful backyard with the... (10 minutes later) ... I remember when my grandmother taught me her secret recipe for brown rice. It was a cold night, the evening before Thanksgiving ... (10 minutes later)... we were talking about that horrible man in Iowa who forced his wife to sign that 'Contract of Wifely Expectations.' Did you see that on TV? If you ever thought about anything like that, mister, I'll... (10 minutes later)... and I was wondering if you think I should put up mauve or black curtains in our den, considering what I told you about them matching the couches?"

Under Inverted Pyramid rule, I could have eradicated world hunger during that time.

Save the world: Practice Inverted Pyramid in your life.

Note: Inverted Pyramid doesn't apply to newspaper columns.

Welcome to Grad-advice-ville. Population: You

From 6-2-99

A recent high school or college graduate can't go to the bathroom without receiving "words of wisdom" from us old folks.

But most of that advice falls along the lines of "be all you can be and you'll go far" or "don't look a gift horse in the mouth," which translated into how it actually affects a high school or college graduate, means absolutely nothing.

Thus, in the interests of mankind, I have put together some tidbits of advice that graduates can actually use. It's my gift to them.

Digest:

• Don't ever say "I'm starving" out loud until you know what's being served.

They may be serving liver-kabobs.

• Trust your instincts.

Unless you're an idiot. In that case, don't trust your instincts.

• Never play cards with someone who has a nickname that includes a major American city – i.e, "Detroit Danny" or "Memphis Mel."

• Personality and your appearance count a great deal.

That doesn't mean you have to be a supermodel. But if you look like a bum, and act like a bum – you're a bum.

• Don't be afraid to speak your mind.

You may find that you regret not saying something more than saying something honest.

• If you have to break up with your significant other, write them a letter. In that letter, simply put: "Dear Baby, Welcome to Dumpsville. Population: You."

• If you get a chance to further your education, do it.

If you don't, you'll regret it the rest of your life. The "real world" isn't as appealing as it looks. Stay a student as long as you can.

• If you have roommates, avoid putting any type of bill in your name.

• Don't make any decisions solely based on love.

• Never give out any personal financial information – i.e., credit card or checking account numbers.

That's a lesson that some of us (most notably, the big, dumb author of this) don't learn until it's too late.

• For those going to college: Live as close to campus as you can. By eliminating obstacles, and excuses, you'll go to class more often.

• Somewhere along the way, befriend a successful lawyer. Someday, you will need them. And even lawyers need friends.

• Make decisions on the way you behave by answering the following:

"If my grandmother saw me doing this, would she approve?"

That may be the best piece of advice you'll ever receive.

Treat an infant like a can of soda
June 16, 1999

Our five-month-old daughter said her first words this week.

She looked right at me and said very loudly, "These pretzels are making me thirsty!"

Oddly enough, she said it in an impeccable British accent. I guess she must be British.

Last week, while my wife was at a training session for her work, I was in a training session with our child, being her primary caregiver (whatever that means) for three days.

When I decided to accept this mission, I envisioned three days of resting on a hotel bed, ordering room service, watching cable television stations that I don't get at home, while our child slept the days away.

What I got was a new-found appreciation for stay-at-home parents and for my talents as an entertainer.

During the course of those three days, we did the usual father-and-daughter bonding stuff: I attempted to teach her how to play poker (until she ate the ace of spades); we watched "Smokey and the Bandit" twice; we re-enacted several scenes from "Punky Brewster" using sock puppets; we laughed and laughed and laughed at our reflections in the mirror (or maybe, she was just laughing at mine).

From this experience, I learned a great deal about infants. If you have one, you may know what I'm talking about. If you are going to have one (most of them come that way), you now have something to dread or look forward to, depending on your outlook.

First, when feeding a child "real food," go ahead and accept the fact that you're going to get messy.

Our child started eating cereal recently, and half of what's in the bowl ends up scattered from head to toe – on the eater and the feeder.

Secondly, I learned that if you jostle around a child for more than a minute, they react just like a can of soda – they inevitably spew a foamy substance in every direction possible.

I also learned that if you watch an infant closely, they do something new – and for the parent, something wondrous – every few hours.

One day, she did some type of bubbling noise with her lips all day long. The next day, she discovered how to sit up by herself. Then, she started doing this thing where she grabs an object and raises it above here head and throws it as far as she can. Moments later, she's learned that when she leaps at a beverage in a glass, the glass topples over and liquid spills on the floor.

Being that I only learned to do those things while in college, I found her progress to be quite remarkable.

Now, she's teaching me that British accent. The learning never stops.

The not-so-secret art of blaming others
July 14, 1999

Everybody makes mistakes.

No one is above erring every once in a while, whether it's not putting the toothpaste lid back on, innocently asking a fat lady when her baby is due, or stealing a sports car.

You might as well accept that you're going to make mistakes and learn from them. As the late, great, unlikely womanizer Benjamin Franklin once said, "It's not whether you make a mistake – it's how you cover it up."

So, even while you may not be perfect, others don't have to know it.

Blaming others when you make a mistake is an art, like ice sculpture, a perfectly-executed double play, or that painting of dogs playing cards. The secret is to spin around any situation where you have been accused of committing a wrong.

Generally, women are the masters of this art form. I learned this early in my marriage.

It would begin with an innocent query while I looked over the phone bill: "Hey, what's this 105-minute phone call to your sister?"

Somehow, a half hour later, I would be apologizing for something I did four months ago.

From that, I learned. Now, instead of being blamed for something I did, I possess the manipulative mojo to turn the simplest of errors into the most victorious of victories.

As a public servant, I am herein listing some tips on how you too can absolve yourself from the gravest of miscues:

• **When accused of something...**

First, accuse the other person of what they accused you of, or of something entirely different, like the Kennedy assassination. When they deny it, say: "If you're so innocent, why don't you admit that you're not?"

When they look around in confusion – run!

You can also act like you don't hear them. I use this all the time at home.

"Honey, did you leave this wet towel on the bathroom floor?"

From the couch, I gurgle "huh?"

"I said – did you leave this wet towel on the bathroom floor?" Her louder tone doesn't penetrate my facade of deafity.

"Huh?"

Repeat until she picks up the towel herself and leaves you alone.

- **When caught lying...**

First of all, you shouldn't lie. But when you do, try these two simple, easy-to-learn sentences to turn the blame around in your favor.

When accused of lying, say: "It takes two to lie. One to lie and one to listen."

Then argue that it's their fault for listening to your lie.

- **When at work...**

There are several ways to get out of trouble at work, depending on the situation.

For general foul-ups or misbehavior, use: "It was like that when I got here," or "I wasn't here. You need to ask (whichever fellow employee doesn't happen to be there at the time)," or "I don't know who was making copies of their butt on the copy machine, but I saw (least favorite co-worker) sitting on the copier with their pants down."

If you can't blame a co-worker, try a customer.

"I'm not one to name names, but I saw Mr. Hogenboom reach into your desk and take all your pens, boss. I was tempted to tackle him, but then I remembered that thing you keep saying about the customer always being right."

- **When you have children...**

Children are a joy. They are especially a joy when they can't speak, and thus, can't defend themselves against baseless accusations.

"Who spilled this on the floor?"

"Uh, the baby did it."

Automatically out of trouble.

Unfortunately, you only have a limited amount of time that will work. Take advantage of it when you have the chance.

Soon, children will learn from you. Then, you'll be in the kind of trouble you can't spin.

How to Avoid Embarrassing Moments, Part One

9-15-99

In my continuing efforts to help mankind, I am starting a series today in this space that will spare you, the reader, much trouble, heartache, and chagrin.

I am calling the series, "How to Avoid Embarrassing Moments."

I consider myself an expert on the subject, having avoided 13 of 72 (18 percent) potentially embarrassing situations in this year alone.

Today, we will focus on Embarrassing Situation #1: What to do when you go the bathroom (unfortunately, #2) in a foreign bathroom and you realize (too late) that there is no toilet paper.

Admit it – everyone has experienced this prickly peccadillo at least once. Except for me, of course.

Unfortunately, the human digestive system operates on its own social calendar, and a visit to an unfamiliar bathroom is a scenario that often can't, for medical reasons, be avoided.

But there's no reason to worry anymore. Here's what to do.

The proper course to take once you realize you are in this position is to:

1. Remain calm.

If you are in a foreign climate, particularly a social gathering or at a restaurant or in a rodeo bathroom, screaming hysterically for toilet paper will only alert others, which will cause them to point and laugh at you once discovered.

Also, for you men, resist your initial primal instinct, which is to grab whatever's handy – like a sock or a copy of Glamour. You can think about it, but don't do it!

2. Look around for a window. Most bathrooms have them.

3. This is the tricky part.

Without soiling yourself unnecessarily, lock the bathroom door and hoist yourself out the window. You may want to check if you are on the first floor or a higher floor before jumping out the window. Sometimes that makes a difference.

4. Once safely on the ground, you have two choices: 4a. You can find some foliage and use that for your purposes (Warning: During the seasonal changes of all, this could be dangerous). Or 4b. You can

flag down a passing motorist and ask them for some toilet paper (Note: At first, they may be hesitant about helping you. But once you fully explain the reason you have your pants around your ankles, some may be glad to help).

5. When you have completed the task, simply go back through the window into the bathroom and return to your shindig in a confident swagger, fully bypassing this potentially embarrassing disaster.

Next in this series: Embarrassing Situation #2: "What to do when you see your mother-in-law naked."

How to Avoid Embarrassing Moments, Parts Two & Three

September 29, 1999

Today, as part of my one-man crusade to save the world, I will continue my series, "How to Avoid Embarassing Moments."

When we last met, I was explaining what do when you see your mother-in-law naked – which I dubbed Embarassing Situation #2. Fortunately, Embarassing Situation #3, which I will unveil shortly, and Embarassing Situation #2 have the same two solutions – which, for the sake of clarity, I will call Solution #1 for Embarassing Situations #2 and #3, and Solution #2 for Embrassing Situations #2 and #3.

Embarassing Situation #3 is one that we absent-minded, idiot savant types run into on the regular basis – calling people by the wrong name.

Sometimes, such a faux pas can be hilarious – like when you mess up on your wedding vows by saying, "I take you, (old girlfriend's name), to be my wedfully awful wife," or when you accidently call your boss by his unbeknownst-to-him nickname of "Napoleon Skinflint."

Everyone gets a kick out of those types of gaffes and hearty guffaws are had by all.

But, other times, mislabeling a person can get downright ugly, and that's when you need to take the proper courses to escape embarassment.

Here's what to do:

Solution #1 – The best way to explain Solution #1 is to give an example. Say you're at some type of social function, or a cockfight, and you see an older, distinguished lady.

"Hey, Mrs. Huffnagle, my, that's a lovely shade of green you're wearing this evening. Put some holes in it and you'd look like a pool table."

"Young man, I am not Mrs. Huffnagle."

At this point, you must make a conscience effort not to react at all, but rather stare intently at an object behind and to the right of the woman you thought to be Mrs. Huffnagle.

Then say, "Why, I'm sorry, I was partially-blinded in a lemon-eating incident recently, and by the illuminating, angelic glow that surrounded you, I thought you to be Mrs. Huffnagle. Please accept my sincerest apologies."

If conversation follows, just go with the flow. But make sure that you keep staring behind her and to the right, and for good effect, trip over a coffee table or a lamp or something as you leave.

If she mentions the "lovely shade of green" remark and questions how you could see that, start coughing profusely, bend over, and hobble away.

This solution, of course, also works for seeing your mother-in-law naked, except don't use the part about the illuminating, angelic glow. That could spell more trouble.

Solution #2 is simple. It's much like Solution #1, except that it's different in a lot of ways.

When faced with these types of situations, slowly lift your hands over your head, start sobbing, and run in the opposite direction as fast as you can, making sure to flail your arms as you run.

I know – flailing is hard – but to escape these types of awkward moments, you have to go the extra mile.

You may now go into the world with the confidence to elude embarassment. You're welcome.

Sure-fire ways to avoid jury duty
October 10, 1999

"Have you ever been convicted of a felony?"

I believe my answer to that query got me relieved from jury duty.

"Convicted...," I said slowly, pausing for an eternity, swirling an imaginary lozenge in my mouth with one eye closed – the official trying-to-remember-my-brushes-with-the-law facial contortion. "Naw, never convicted."

Five times out of 10, which is almost 50 percent, the above dialogue will exempt you from jury duty.

Almost one percent of Americans will be called for jury duty this year alone. Ironically, that's the same percentage of Americans that vote. I have no idea why I was called for jury duty last week. I assume since my wife was also summoned, the jury pool was chosen out of the "Rs" in the phone book. That makes sense.

Anyway, contrary to its name, jury duty is not a duty, but rather a privilege. That's what I've been told. Apparently, "jury privilege" just doesn't sound right.

Regardless, for those of you who have a last name that starts with "S" – you're next.

I don't in any way condone using ploys, trickery or deception to absolve yourself from the jury privilege, but fellow inmates have told me that the following are sure-fire methods to spare yourself from being a juror:

• When they ask you if you know the defendant, reply: "No, but he looks just like the maggot that stole my post-hole digger."

• Enter the courtroom. Sit down. Then jump up and scream "I object!"

Sit back down.

Repeat every two minutes until you are apprehended.

• When an attorney asks if there is anything that would prejudice you against a defendant (or an attorney), answer "Yes!" very loudly.

When they ask you what would prejudice you, say: "I don't know. He just looks like a crook."

• Sometime after being seated as a potential juror, raise your hand. When acknowledged, ask: "Is this a death penalty case?"

If they answer yes, yell "Yippee!" immediately and attempt to give a fellow juror a high five. If they answer no or I don't know or something other than yes, react with disgust and bellow, "Darn! Man, I wanted to fry someone!"

• When seated as a potential juror, go to the front row. Then raise your hand and ask: "May I go to the bathroom?"

When someone replies affirmatively, stare straight ahead with a determined glare for about a minute, as if you're straining. Squint your eyes and furrow your brow. Then let out a loud sigh, look at whoever gave you permission to use the bathroom, and say, "Thank you."

• When asked what your occupation is, respond, "I work for a newspap..."

"You're excused."

I wonder why that always works.

The inherent evil of men's bicycle design
February 16, 2000

Call me easily confused, or Mel, but I can't make heads or sense of tails and things that... oh, never mind.

Maybe my common sense is rather uncommon, but there is a lot in our society that just doesn't seem right to me.

For instance, I find that still having an electoral college is a slap to the face of convention. The fact that the Canadian Football League has two teams nicknamed the Roughriders is an atomic wedgie to reason. And I regard Garth Brooks' immense popularity as a kick in the shin to logic.

But this week I remembered the lowest blow to rationality – quite literally.

What I'm talking about, Willis, is the nonsensical sexuality of bicycles. Let me rephrase that. It's the way bicycles are made for the differing sexes.

Women's bicycles are made with a bar heading from the steering wheel column down to the chain area – at a downward angle. Men's bicycles have a bar going straight from the steering wheel column across to the bar holding up the seat.

Why is this a problem? Why do I consider the design of men's bicycles to not only make no sense whatsoever, but also be a nightmarish danger?

Let me tell you one man's story that almost wasn't a man's story.

One day, when I was about 13 or so, I was riding a 10-speed bicycle made in the men's style with the bar going straight across. I was riding along, minding my own business, thinking about Pac-Man, when I hit a very large pothole. The front tire stopped, and the ugliness of the momentum surged my body forward.

That's where I met the cruelty of the men's bicycle bar.

As many of you men know, when hit in your most precious of areas, the pain teases you. It waits a few seconds after the initial shock – then, as you cringe in a ghostly white horror, it turns every nerve ending in your body into a chorus of jellyfish stings.

I somehow got off my bicycle and struggled to a nearby bathroom, where I did a rudimentary exam to determine if I was still a boy. I was – barely.

As I walked my bicycle back home, knock-kneed and still in a cold sweat, I cursed the design of this instrument of castration, wondering what they were thinking. In the same circumstance, if I had a women's bicycle, with the bar going downward, I may have had time to react and avoid the agony.

Fast forward to this past weekend. My wife and father put a baby seat on my wife's bicycle. I supervised from the couch.

"Len, why don't you get a man's bike and you can ride the baby around too," my wife suggested.

My neck twitched as the memory of my date with the man's bike bar flashed through my mind.

"Nope, I don't think so," I said, jumping on her bike, the dreaded bar a good foot from the seat. "I think I'll be riding this one."

Call me a girl – I don't care. I'm riding the bike that men should be riding.

Perplexed by the female packing formula
February 23, 2000

It took me 35 minutes to pack for a five-day honeymoon.

My future wife had to take two days off of work.

That should have given me a clue.

Since that point, the time it takes my wife to pack for even the simplest of journeys has perplexed me, puzzled me, and put me at wit's end – which isn't very far.

What makes the length of this otherwise seemingly uncomplicated process so troublesome? It makes no sense. In other arenas much more treacherous, she is the queen of time management.

Sunday morning, she takes a shower, makes breakfast, feeds our child, washes dishes, dresses the child and herself for church, makes lunch, vacuums the living room, reads a book to our child, and wakes me up twice – all in an hour-and-a-half.

But an overnight trip to her grandmother's takes four hours for her to pack one bag of clothes.

And for some reason, I must assist in this tortuous process – a reluctant Igor to her mad packing doctor.

"When do you want to leave tomorrow?" She asks Friday night at 9 p.m. about an overnight visit to her father's in Albany on Saturday.

"Oh, I guess around 10 a.m. or so," I reply, relaxing on the couch after a hard week of work.

"What are you doing sitting around then? We've got to get ready," she barked in a panic. "You've got to help me pack. We've got to start now."

She then heads into her closet in a rush, mumbling something grumpily. For the next 15 minutes, all I see are clothes flying out of the closet as the grumpy mumbles continue.

Why is it this way? I could understand spending hours on packing if she were taking an ungodly Zsa Zsa Gabor-amount of clothes with her wherever she went, but that's not the case. She only overpacks ridiculously – like every other woman on the planet.

But why does it take so long?

Like Jordan against the Clippers, or me against a pizza buffet, you can't stop it, or even explain it. You can only hope to contain it.

Thus, I started doing research, four years of it, and with the help of a calculator, a number two-and-a-half pencil, and a pound of Bryl Cream, I came up with the following formula so that, at the least, I could safely predict how long it will take for my wife to pack.

The formula is: Total hours the trip will take (including ride) divided by six = hours it will take to pack.

Using this formula, a one-day sojourn, leaving at 5 p.m. Friday and returning home at 5 p.m. Saturday, takes her four hours to pack.

Right on the money.

Me? Takes 11 minutes.

My formula: Total minutes it takes to put proper amount of clothing, supplies, etc. in bag + nothing = total minutes it will take to pack.

Let's hope I don't have to test my formula using all of my stuff.

Toothbrush mishap? Call the HELPLINE
March 22, 2000

I may be the only man in American to admit that – sometimes – I need directions.

I need directions when I'm assembling any type of children's toy or device. I need directions when I'm assembling any type of adult's toy or device. And I especially need directions when I'm driving in a place I've never been before and I've received directions from a woman.

But there are some things that just don't require directions – even for me and my fellow simpletons.

I came to this realization recently via the one item that rarely brings such epiphanies – the toothbrush.

I'm not one to give toothbrushes, or teeth, or math, much thought. But at some point, my wife was apparently told by a deranged dentist that you must purchase a new toothbrush with every tube of toothpaste. We have less oxygen going in and out of our house than we have toothbrushes. They're all over the place.

I happened upon the newest additions to our toothbrush family the other day, still wrapped in its fancy little package.

Being bored in the bathroom usually leads to bloodshed (see 1994's Shaving Chest Incident), but this time, I chose to read the toothbrush box.

On the box, the following was written:

DIRECTIONS: Take toothbrush from box, using the exit at the top. To use toothbrush, place toothpaste on top of toothbrush bristles, not on the side. Place toothbrush in mouth, moving bristles in a side-to-side motion against the enamel of your teeth. Brush rigorously, then rinse mouth. Repeat.

Then at the bottom of the directions, the following was written: HELPLINE: If you have problems using this toothbrush, please call our 24-hour HELPLINE at...

It then went on to list a 1-800 number for the HELPLINE. Yes, a toothbrush with its own directions, and a 1-800 HELPLINE (so important is has to be capitalized).

Now, I could understand needing to have directions to use a toothbrush for a one-year-old infant, or an adult who has been raised by apes in the jungle and has just been returned to civilization.

But, usually – and I know I'm jumping to conclusions here – one-year-olds and ape-men just released into civilized society can't read.

This piqued my interest.

I mean, what kind of toothbrush emergencies can one have that would require 24-hour 1-800 number assistance?

"Yes, I'm placing the toothpaste on the brush, but it keeps falling off the bristles before it goes into my mouth! What am I to do?! Help! God save me from this horror!"

"Hold it, sir. First, calm down. Take a deep breath. This is not a life-or-death situation – yet."

We don't even have a 911 system here, yet there's a 24-hour hotline for people who can't operate a manual toothbrush.

As stated, I need directions to open a can of soup, but even I don't need directions on how to operate a toothbrush. On the times I miss my mouth and stick the toothbrush in my eye, I usually just quit and try again the next day.

Who needs directions for that?

Census-filling-outing made easy by math
March 29, 2000

This month, literally hundreds of Americans will be filling out Census 2000 forms.

As is my weekly custom, I am here to help.

This past Thursday, I took the day off to complete my census form. After an arduous nine hours, more than one temper tantrum, and finally, a group family hug, I presented my completed census form to my doctor.

So, as an experienced census filler-outer, I am here to give you a few tips. They are, in alphabetical order:

1. Prior to starting, have a big, hearty breakfast.

Your mind thinks better if you aren't hungry, and you're probably going to need your strength. Doing some calisthenics is also a good idea.

B. Make sure you are prepared.

I would suggest having the following within reaching distance prior to starting the census-filling-outing process: Some type of refreshing cold drink, like Fresca; four to nine colorful writing utensils (I used a flesh-colored crayon and some pink hi-liters); a thesaurus; a thorough written history of your family genealogy; a calculator; a used copy of "I'm OK, You're OK;" some handkerchiefs; and a full can of breath spray (breath mints will do in a pinch).

3. Ignore the part about name and address.

4. Once you are done with that, you are now ready for the most important part of the census – counting the people that live in your household.

This is by far the most integral part of the census-filling-outing. How many people live in your household determines how your community will be represented in our government, how much money your community will receive in governmental assistance, how much your phone bill will be each month, how many channels will be offered by your cable television system, and how frequently your garbage is picked up.

Thus, to improve our community, and to get my garbage picked up once a week – the more people, the better.

What I did was think of the number of people that actually *could* live in my house. We only have three people living in our house, but we have nine rooms, not including closets. I figured that we could probably fit about five people per room comfortably.

With that in mind, I used the following formula to determine the number of people I would write on my census form that live in our household: Number of rooms in my house (9) multiplied by the number of people that could fit comfortably in each room (5) = 67.

I suggest you utilize the same mathematical formula for the best results.

5. Go the extra mile.

There is a lot of information that the census form doesn't ask for, but that our government needs to know to make this year's census complete. On the back of your census form, make sure to write down any other information that you feel is irrelevant.

For instance, I wrote a short story about my hobbies, dogs I've owned during my life, why I prefer Captain D's over Long John Silver's, and a first-person account of the autobiography of Mr. T.

If you need more room for this part of the census, use extra sheets of paper, then staple them to the lower right-hand corner of your census form.

Remember, census-filling-out is your duty as an American or illegal alien. If there is one thing you've learned from this inspirational column, I hope it's that we all must be counted even if we can't count.

Bless his heart, he comes from Yankees
April 12, 2000

Ever been around a bunch of Yankees?

God bless them, but they aren't much for tact. Or soap either.

It is my belief that somewhere in the genetic process, Yankees breeding with Yankees have caused a phenomenon where they have lost the ability to send a message from their nerve endings to their brains. Instead, all impulses go straight from their nerve endings to their mouths.

Being that a small minority of my long-gone ancestors are from the North (woops!), I sometimes slip up (just illustrated) and put my mouth in gear before my brain is even cranked up. Many of my readers would add that this affliction also applies to my columns.

It's taken generations of Southernization, but I'm almost immune from the Yankee inbreeding that caused this genetic mutation.

But just because Southerners appear tactful and respectful doesn't mean that they are above being critical or downright mean-spirited.

Listen to a bunch of Southern ladies speak. Listen closely, very closely. They have found a way, through just turning a phrase, of blasting someone to smithereens while sounding sweet as sugar.

"Did you hear about that poor, poor Minnie Tilton?"

The other ladies shake their heads with a chorus of "no's."

"Oh, that poor Minnie. You know she's had a problem with her weight for so long. Can't put down a fried chicken leg to save her soul. Anyway, she was at her son's wedding last week – you know the one who, God bless him, has teeth that look like bamboo stalks – when she bent down to pick up a handkerchief, and split her $500 dress right in two. Showed her backside, which, bless her heart, is as big as my washing machine, to God and everybody. Some awful gentleman said he saw harpoon marks, bless her heart."

What the above illustrates is that Southern women have found a method to circumnavigate all rules of Southern etiquette and say whatever they want and still sound diplomatic.

The way to walk the tact tightrope is by prefacing everything nasty with "bless her (or his) heart" or "God bless him (or her), or by referring to a person as "poor, poor (name of victim)" prior to slandering them.

For example, insert the above phrases in their proper places for the sentence: "Johnny Joe Jones was so drunk he couldn't fish."

The delicate, Southern way of uttering that sentence is: "That poor, poor Johnny Joe Jones, bless his heart, was so drunk he couldn't fish."

You feel sorry for the guy, don't you?

Zipping up is not as easy as X-Y-Z
June 21, 2000

There has been a lot of debate lately among media types about how dangerous guns are.

Guns, shmuns.

For the male gender, a weapon that is far more dangerous than any gun can be found right on their person – at nearly all times, in the most vulnerable of places.

What I'm talking about is the most underrated weapon of all time – the zipper.

How is an innocent ole zipper dangerous, you ask?

Let me enlighten you; then frighten you.

In our topsy-turvy, fast-paced, instant-grits, instant-pudding world, you're always thinking, always on the go. You have to be just to keep up.

The zipper wasn't built with that in mind. For if you are a man – and you have a zipper – and you, in your haste to zip up your pants and get on with the quick pace of life – lose your concentration for one iota of a second – it's "Hello, Soprano." Just like that.

The zipper's supposed purpose is to provide an easy way to fasten and unfasten your pants. The zipper is constructed with numerous jagged teeth of pain that go up to fasten, and down to unfasten.

My main problem with the zipper is the "jagged teeth of pain" part. Having jagged teeth of pain in close proximity to parts of my body which can withstand no amount of pain whatsoever is at best short-sighted – at worst, downright evil.

Another issue I have with the zipper is its reliability. In that area of my person, I need absolute dependability. For some insane reason, society frowns upon a man walking into a room of mixed company with his fly open.

And in my experience, zippers aren't 100 percent reliable in that regard (see wedding rehearsal party, 1996).

A while back, button-fly pants came into the public consciousness, and easily-distracted men everywhere breathed a sigh of relief so strong that it started an avalanche in Peru. But, alas, that fad faded, and now, button-fly pants are about as easy to find as a basset hound in Beijing.

I've looked into other options.

My wife has some pants with the zipper on the side. Sounded like a great idea. One day, when she was gone, I lowered the shades and tried them on. Didn't have much room, though. I also immediately started rearranging furniture in our living room for no good reason, and suddenly found HGTV utterly appealing.

After taking them off, I immediately came to my senses, changed the channel to ESPN and went to the bathroom and left the toilet seat up.

My attention was distracted for a second as I zipped up. Another catastrophe avoided.

There's got to be a better way.

Down on America?
Go to a high school football game
August 30, 2000

In this political season, we hear a lot about what is wrong with America.

On Friday night, though, I will be sitting in the stands of a high school football game – and sometime during the contest, I'll look around, soak in the atmosphere with a deep breath, exhale, and then smile.

During that four-second moment, I will come to the conclusion that, while there are indeed some problems in our country, we are still blessed to live in the greatest country the world has ever known.

What do I see in that four seconds at a high school football game that brings me to that realization?

I'm glad I asked.

I see the the kid way too small to be on a varsity football team, 115 pounds soaking wet, who, because one of his bigger, more mature teammates gets hurt, is thrust onto the field and away from the comfort of the sidelines. As he runs confusedly on the field, not knowing what in the world he's supposed to do, the helmet that is way too big for his head shifts sideways, and he runs to the huddle as fast as his skinny legs can muster looking through his earhole.

I see the meek, overweight kid who is blowing a mean trumpet during the halftime show, beaming as he leaves the field, proud of his performance, enjoying the camaraderie he and his bandmates share.

I see the talented football player make great play after great play. Due to his football talents, this young man may get a college football scholarship. He could be the first person in his family to be able to go to college. In that process, he can better himself and his family's lot in life through his education and the benefits it provides.

I see the not-so-talented football player who makes great play after great play.

He won't go to college on a football scholarship. He may not go to college at all. He will, though, learn some valuable lessons through his experiences, and derive enough glory and good memories to last a lifetime.

I see the cheerleader on the sideline, cheering for her peers like crazy, enjoying herself so much that she doesn't notice when the other team returns an interception 90 yards for a touchdown.

I see the group of little boys off in the dark recesses of the stadium, playing their own game of football using a tattered popcorn cup. Just when it looks like one of them is going to score by crossing the goal line marked by Todd's shirt and a Coke bottle, Billy's mother breaks up the game to scold him about tearing his new jeans.

I see the ladies and gentlemen in the concession stand, sweating to feed the hungry masses, finally getting a break when the game turns tense late in the third quarter. Their hard work is not rewarded by financial gain – there is none – but rather by the knowledge that their efforts are helping their community's children.

I see the other volunteers too – the ones who spend every Friday night selflessly helping out where they can. These people won't make the Saturday morning boxscore, but they are the real Friday night heroes.

I see the smile on the coach's face when the kid who has missed his blocking assignment 50 times in practice absolutely aces it during a game. That coach had stayed after practice with the kid to teach him the proper technique.

I see one community coming together, putting their boys against your boys, their community versus yours. It's not white against black, rich against poor. It's ours against yours in a game whose stakes have nothing to do with money, but rather to do with a little community pride and a lot of fun.

A community can be poor. It can be ugly. But on Friday night, it can field a good football team, a loud, finely-tuned band, with energetic cheerleaders and frenzied fans, and feel real good about itself.

I see that as a good thing.

Want to feel good about America? Go to a high school football game. You'll see it too.

Having trouble sleeping? Read this column
September 13, 2000

On certain occasions – like when the Georgia Bulldogs lose a football game they should have won by 40 points – I can't seem to go to sleep.

I am not alone.

According to Penthouse magazine, 5 out of 3 American citizens and illegal aliens have trouble sleeping.

What they suffer from is insomnia – a prolonged and abnormal inability to obtain adequate sleep. The medical community has a name for those who suffer from this ailment – sleepy people.

I am not one of the sleepy people, but I feel their weariness. There are many a morning when I wake up groggy, not having received the minimal amount of sleep. I'm just no good all day if I don't get my 10 hours a night.

But, once again, I am here to help. As a public servant, I have done extensive research on the plight of sleepy people, and have come up with a number of ways to assist them in their search for dreamland.

Showing my devotion to you, the sleepy reader, I personally attempted each of these snooze-induction tactics, putting the needs of you, the sleepy reader, ahead of my own personal safety.

You're welcome in advance.

Below sleepy readers will find some supposed insomnia-curing remedies, with my own personal grade on how effective they were.

The Sleepy Sounds alarm clock: My mother visited us this past week, and swears by this alarm clock/radio thingy that plays soothing, sleep-inducing sounds at bedtime.

Among the sounds are waves crashing on the beach, wind rustling through the trees, a light thunderstorm, a heavy rain shower, Walter Mondale doing an oral interpretation of "My Cousin Vinny," and a play-by-play announcer calling action from a 0-0 soccer match.

My grade: A. Put me to sleep right away. Didn't even get to hear Mondale's dead-on impersonation of Marisa Tomei.

Counting sheep: I've tried this a couple of times, and it works for me. All I do is count to 10 and I'm gone (Warning: Doesn't work for residents of Alabama).

My grade: A.

NyQuil: According to the bottle, an adult is supposed to take one teaspoon and it's snooze city.

Thus, I took half a teaspoon and didn't go to sleep right away. Being the patient type, I waited a couple of minutes and took two more teaspoons. To my surprise, I wasn't asleep, but rather found myself wandering around the house talking aloud about pancakes.

Not nearly asleep and now wearing a Santa Claus hat, I figured I just needed a heavier dosage and took three more teaspoons. This led to me singing TV theme songs while playing bongos in my yard. After the police came, I still wasn't asleep.

So I decided to order a pizza and drank the rest of the bottle.

I went to sleep alright. And woke up the next day in the laundry room with no shirt on, an empty bag of Doritos on my chest, crumbs all in my hair, with a javelin under my arms, and still clutching the empty bottle of NyQuil in my hand.

My grade: A+.

Think about politics: This is my personal get-to-sleep method.

I just start thinking about political things I have forgotten from Mr. Shirk's class in middle school, like trying to recall presidential campaign slogans. For instance, I remember "Tippecanoe and Tyler Too," "Me Loves Millard," "Chester A. Arthur or Bust," "I Like Ike," and by the time I get to "George W. Bush: He's As Smart As We Is," I'm snoring.

My grade: A+ (Gets A+ because I made it up.)

So, sleepy people, rejoice! As is my custom, I have given you four sure-fire methods to relieve your fatigue and have fruitful, rested lives.

Happy Sleeping!

Having a free barber has its own price
September 27, 2000

It is one of my personal goals in life to never pay over $10 (with tip) for a haircut.

Sticking to that goal has its own price, though.

When my barber, Mac Smith, passed away 10 months ago, many of us local menfolk found ourselves in dire straits.

Like many women who prefer their "female doctors" to be female, I prefer my man hair to be cut by a man – in a real barber shop.

My preference has nothing to do with sexism. It has everything to do with economics. It is contended that women make 50 cents for every dollar a man makes in the workplace. It is my contention that women make up that deficit by charging a dollar for every 50 cents that a male barber charges for a haircut.

Thus, I was in a quandary. I could forsake everything I believed in and pay $12 for a $6 haircut, or I could drive 40 miles to the Baytree Barber Shop in Valdosta.

As is my custom when faced with a life-altering decision, I turned to my wife.

She gleefully volunteered to be my personal barber – at no charge.

But what I've learned in the resulting 10 months is that there is a price to pay for having your own female, personal barber who happens to be your wife – sometimes an ugly one.

That price is paid by your appearance – depending on the barber's mood. The quality of my haircut is directly proportional to how happy or mad my wife/barber is with me at that exact moment.

I never seemed to have that problem with Mac. But then again, I was paying him.

When my wife is happy with me, like after I've washed dishes or handed her a wad of cash, my haircuts seem to go fine. There are no gaping holes, the sideburns are almost even, and I look like a well-coiffed hobo.

But on other occasions, like right after I leave a series of wet towels on the carpet for no apparent reason, I come out of our haircutting sessions looking like someone had burned my hair off.

After a few of those haircuts, I know what to look for now.

I now jump out of the chair if: A. She starts laughing for no reason as she is cutting my hair; or B. She is mumbling something like, "I'll show you to put down the toilet seat..." as I see clumps of hair falling all over the torso.

This past week, it was haircut time again, and everything seemed to be going smoothly. I saw none of the tell-tale signs of hair-cutting vengeance, and only received two skin-breaking wounds.

But then I looked in the mirror. Apparently, I murdered her grandmother and forgot about it, because on the left side of my forehead, my bangs were about a quarter-inch long, while on the right side, hair was falling down about six inches, down to my eyebrows.

That type of haircut is fine if I were the bassist for "A Flock of Seagulls" in 1984, but it doesn't work if I'm planning on going outside in 2000.

"What have I done?" I asked pathetically to my wife, as my 21-month-old daughter looked up at her father, pointed at my head, and started laughing hysterically, screaming, "Daddy look goofy! Daddy look goofy!"

My wife assured me that I had done nothing to make her mad. She had just made a slight mistake in cutting my bangs.

Hey, you get what you pay for.

There's a skeeter on my heater – Get it off!
October 4, 2000

It landed on my arm as light as a feather boa as worn by William "Refrigerator" Perry.

Upon initial glance, I deduced that the perpetuator of the thud was either a giant mosquito or a blood-sucking crow.

My usual reaction to a mosquito on my person is to lightly slap in the vicinity of the pest, either "shooing" it away or smashing it to smithereens. On this occasion, though, that didn't work.

I was surprised to find the mosquito was still on my arm, glaring up at me as if to say, "Quit bothering me."

I then unleashed a hellish slap toward the beast that I usually reserve for the guy at the card table I find cheating. This seemed to stun the mosquito, causing him to stagger a little before regaining his composure. He looked up at me with bloodshot eyes, obviously from a long night drinking, and gave me a deflated look that said, "okay, I get the picture," and flew off to swallow some infant whole.

Here in South Georgia, we are used to an annual, year-long deluge of mosquitoes, but the recent rains from Tropical Storm Helene have awakened a furious, thirsty flock bent on making up for lost time after a dry, dormant summer.

For me to whine at all about what we call "skeeters" means they are a serious problem indeed.

First, I was born with the thick skin of a newspaper editor. When I give blood, it usually takes three trained medical professionals and a special, blood-seeking, blue lamp to find a vein. Blood-sucking insects usually give my skin a brief inspection and move on.

Secondly, I'm from South Georgia, and am accustomed to mosquitoes and heat, and more mosquitoes and heat. All of us have had visitors at one time or another who have complained about our bugs. I never really knew what they were talking about until this past week. One weekend many years ago, I brought my college roommate home with me for Easter. I don't want to embarrass this person by identifying him by name, but Cale Conley was not fond of our skeeters. When my family was outside on the deck enjoying Easter dinner, Cale stayed indoors.

"Cale, don't you want to come outside and get something to eat?" I asked him, concerned that he was feeling left out.

"No," he said, wrapped in a blanket on the couch with a panty on his head.

"Why not?"

"I'm scared of the mosquitoes," he said with a shiver. "One of them made me bleed."

I chalked up his fears to being one of those thin-skinned city folk, but now I feel his pain.

For the past week, I have shunned the outdoors. When my family and I pull into our carport, we have been reduced to fleeing from our car and running in a huddled mass to the back door of the house, as if some sniper was peppering us with gunfire from the woods.

Once inside, it's still bad. Twice last week, I heard a knock on my door around 8:15 p.m., and was foolish enough to answer it. The second I opened the door, a swarm of merry mosquito pranksters flew in to ravage every pore in our bodies. The neighborhood dogs have been disappearing at any alarming rate, as have pot roasts.

I've tried shooting them with a pistol, but my wife didn't like that too much. Something about hitting the microwave oven and china cabinet soured her on gunplay in the house for some odd reason.

I wonder how much one of those skeeter trucks costs?

'What's that?' It's a new way of learning
November 29, 2000

Twenty-month-old girls will fall for anything.

My daughter's latest utterance, repeated about, oh, every nanosecond, is "What's that?"

The game goes as follows: She points at an object and says "What's that?" When I explain what "that" is, she moves on to the next object in rapid-fire succession until everything in her peripheral range is covered.

At first, I could keep up.

She pointed at the television. "What's that?"

"That's a television. It will be your friend throughout life. Embrace it. Love it. Watch it," was my reply.

She pointed at the couch. "What's that?"

"That's a couch. If your daddy is lying there, you are not to bother him for any reason with the exceptions being: You are choking on something really big; or there's a fire that's directly threatening your daddy's person."

She pointed at the fireplace. "What's that?"

"That's a fireplace. It's hot. You never need to play in there. And if daddy catches on fire while playing in there, please call the fire department by using the phone."

"What's that?"

You get the picture.

But after receiving numerous explanations about the major items in our household, outdoors, and in every children's book in our home, she moved up and on.

She pointed to the small box at the bottom of the wall where a bunch of telephone wires were coming out. "What's that?"

"Uh, that's a box with a bunch of telephone wires coming out of it that does, uh, something, and the wires, go to phones so we can, hmm, call people on the phones. Yeah, that's right."

She gave me that perplexed look usually reserved for when a stuffed toy talks to her.

She pointed to the piece of fabric looped around the back of my tennis shoes. "What's that?"

"That's, well, that's a thing on the back of my shoe," I said as confidently as I would when discussing how electricity works.

Again, the talking stuffed toy look.

Finally, after being stumped a couple of hundred times, and sounding like a Florida graduate attempting to explain subtraction, I had an epiphany.

She doesn't know anything. That's why she's been asking me all these questions. Aha!

I was properly prepared for our next session in curiosity.

She pointed at the child-proof device that covers the empty electric socket so that she doesn't end up with hair like Don King. "What's that?"

"That, my dear, is a mucklelack."

She didn't seem convinced. I decided I needed to fully explain my explanations. There's no use in wasting my massive intellect when I need to learn the child.

"It was discovered by the ancient Inca Indians in 1979. It's made of 100 percent pure peanut butter."

Satisfied, she pointed at the bouncy door-stop thingy with the white top on the end of it. "What's that?"

"That's a Tammy. Invented by Sir Isaac Newton in 1962, and named in honor of his sister, Tammy."

She then ran into the bathroom, where she pointed at the empty cardboard toilet paper tube. "What's that?"

"That's a perplunk. Astronaut Phyllis Diller discovered the perplunk on her 1909 mission to Alabama in search of intelligent life. The perplunk is all she found."

Now learned, she wandered off into the kitchen to play in the trash.

I guess it's okay to fall for anything when you're 20 months old. It's 20 years old that causes problems.

The right excuse can correct any mistake
December 27, 2000

"Ya'll spelled my aunt's name wrong."

The caller was referring to an obituary that had appeared in our newspaper. Apparently, we had spelled the name of one of the many survivors, this man's aunt, incorrectly.

As is our custom, I apologized profusely, and asked if he would like us to print the obituary again.

"Yes," the man said. "But ya'll spelled my aunt's name wrong."

"Yes, sir, I understand," I replied, surveying the very long obituary in question. "But look at all the names we spelled right."

While there are no excuses for such an error, the above is one of my personal favorites.

I have adopted it as my excuse mantra at the homestead.

"Len, look at all the leaves you dragged in from outside," my wife said, pointing to the trail of yard refuse in my wake as I entered our dwelling.

"Yeah, but I took the garbage out without spilling a drop," was my retort.

"Len, you left the water running in the sink again," she said exhaustedly.

"Yeah, but I didn't bring home any smelly dogs today," was my feeble, yet effective, reply.

"Len, why didn't you pay our power bill like I told you?"

"Uh, well, but I paid the cable bill. At least we can watch TV," I said amid the darkness, pressing the buttons on the remote control furiously to no avail.

"Len, was it you that set the drapes on fire?"

"I don't know, but I washed the dishes twice this week, and only broke that plate your great-grandmother left you."

When you're inherently lazy, you must keep score. Otherwise, you may have to actually work. So what little work you do must be documented and catalogued for those occasions where you do set the drapes on fire for no reason.

The "yeah, but I did something else that was right" excuse can also be used in the workplace, but only on certain occasions. It doesn't seem to work as well with the boss as the spouse. I assume that's because the boss didn't recite any vows before a minister when he hired you. Hmm... (Note to Len: Get boss to recite vows in front of minister so he won't fire you).

At work, I prefer the "it was that way when I got here" method, as in:

"Len, this headline is misspelled! It's supposed to say 'City getting rid of excess parts.' It's misspelled so that it sounds like they are getting rid of excess human gas. Did you type in this headline?"

"It was like that when I got here," is my reply, glancing three quick times in the direction of another person in the room to suggest they were responsible. If he doesn't get that, I usually point at them and clear my throat loudly.

Face it – everybody makes mistakes. But, by just using a little creativity, we don't have to be blamed for them. Leave that to others.

Even you can write a bad newspaper column
January 3, 2001

Often, people approach me and ask, "How do you come up with that stuff you write in your column?"

Before I can answer, they answer: "Are you a drunk?"

While drunkenness helps, it is certainly not the most important component in writing a column that stirs the soul, mind, heart, and wallet of the reader.

Really, it's fairly simple. No writing or intellectual prowess is needed. As shown by me, any idiot can write a somewhat-readable column by following these four easy steps:

1. Find a topic.

The more controversial, the better.

When considering a topic, look for the hot-button issues of the day – something that will engage your reader and jump-start the dialogue around the water cooler. Some examples of topics sure to spark controversy: "What's the Difference Between Catsup and Ketchup?", "The Yumminess of Cheese," "The Shakespearian Legacy of Al Molinaro," or "Rain: Pros and Cons."

2. Take your stand.

Once you've got a topic, you need to make a point. Don't be afraid to be bold. You need to take a strong stance that will either make your reader glad, mad, sad, or a tad repulsed – doesn't matter which.

Often, when faced with a perplexing subject, I find it easier to take both sides of an argument. For instance, if your topic is something dangerously contentious, like "Running Around With Scissors," open your column by stating that running with scissors in your hand is very dangerous. Follow up your point with examples. Then, toward the end of the column, state that while running with scissors is indeed dangerous, it can also be a lot of fun. End by telling a joke about llamas playing cards.

By hitting both sides of a debate, you will please everyone.

3. Jazz it up.

Normal people get tired of reading after a couple of sentences, so you must do something to keep them interested and awake.

An easy way to do that is throw in some curse words, but that may get you fired.

I have found two non-cursing ways to jar the reader from their slumber and get them back on track: A. Throw in a sentence that makes absolutely no sense; or B. Insert an obscure pop-culture reference.

Say your topic is "Cleaning Your Ears: What the Doctors Won't Tell You." Here's how I would include both A. and B. simultaneously to jolt and fascinate the reader:

Cleaning your ears isn't much fun, but is rather important if you want to hear well. Two llamas, a priest, and Al Molinaro ("Al" from "Happy Days") were sitting in a bar when the Pope walked in. That has nothing to do with ears, although Al had fairly big ones. Contrary to what doctors will tell you, the size of your ears has little to do with how well you hear. It does, however, indicate how long you will live.

See – the first sentence lulled you to sleep, while the second one absolutely knocked you to the floor (you may get up now). The reader is then hooked, and will read the rest of the column, waiting for another wacky, inane reference.

4. Close on a positive note.

No matter what your topic, finish with a crowd-pleasing flourish. For instance, if your topic is "How I Hate Mimes," a proper close would be:

In conclusion, mimes have no use on this Earth and possess no entertainment value, and thus, should be banished.

But today was filled with sunshine.

Happy caroling!

See. Wasn't that easy?

Happy writing!

Neighborhood cats a smelly, formidable foe
January 24, 2001

They are my Road Runner.

Like Wile E. Coyote, I am repeatedly foiled in my attempts to combat these pests that have terrorized my territory.

But these aren't your usual dimwitted, harmless household pests – ala mice, roaches, termites or Peeping Toms. For these varmints, there is no licensed exterminator, no restraining orders.

And thus, for me, no relief from their habitual harassment.

They are cats.

They are house cats from other houses – beloved pets who probably purr and play and act nice when they are in their own homes. But for some reason, they have decided that my yard is their refuge for kitty delinquency, foul-smelling debauchery and animal husbandry.

The cat problem didn't become catastrophic (pun intended) until recently. Apparently, a singles bar for kitties opened on my property sometime in the last two months. We don't have any cats, so I have no idea what lured them to my carport (where I believe most of the late-night partying occurs). But about every other morning, we see, or rather smell, the results of their feline felonious festivities.

First, it was in my car. I happily bounced to my auto one morning, eager to greet a bright, sunshiny day. Seconds after I turned the key, it hit me like a pound of Limburger cheese hits Alfalfa – the putrid aroma of urine.

After an internal probe of the auto, I concluded that a perpetrator had urinated directly into my air vents, which in turn, sent the offensive odor swirling through the car when started. Naturally, I immediately accused my two-year-old daughter of being the culprit (she has a history of urinating on things belonging to me – like whatever shirt I'm wearing). Under intense inquisition, her alibi checked out.

My wife (another suspect at the time) then informed me that the smell that overwhelmed my car, and anyone within a square mile of it, was not that of humans, but of cat urine.

Aha! I'm glad I thought of that.

Incident #2 was our home.

While out of town one weekend, we came home to find that our home smelled like a kitty Port-a-Potty. An exhaustive probe ensued, and using the investigative skills honed from years of watching "Scooby Doo," I came to the conclusion that a cat had somehow urinated on our air vents under the house, circulating its funk into every room of our home during the duration of our weekend-long hiatus.

Either all of our air vents (car and home) are made of cat nip, or I have really angered these cats in some way.

Next came my wife's car.

The hit occurred last week, while she was out of town. That's their M.O. – like a gang of wayward teens looking for a wild time, they wait until we're out of town to pee all over everything we own.

Then came this Monday morning – garbage day.

I awoke to find that the garbage that I had put inside the can Sunday night was littered throughout our yard. Such vandalism is usually the workings of the neighborhood cat's natural foe – the neighborhood dog. But while picking up the wet refuse in the freezing cold, I smelled it – the unmistakable stench of the enemy.

They were here. And they were laughing at me.

Does anybody have an Acme catalog? I need a catapult, an anvil and some dynamite.

You may be lazy if: You don't read this
March 7, 2001

I'm lazy.

I had to stick my finger in an electric socket just to force myself off the couch to write this (Note to self: Move computer to couch).

I like being lazy. If I wasn't lazy, I would probably have to get up more often. I've gotten up plenty of times. It's overrated.

You may be lazy too. In between naps, I have compiled a list of 14 things that show whether you are lazy if they apply to you (Why 14? Because I was too lazy to come up with 15. Quit asking stupid questions).

Here goes.

You may be lazy if:

• You have already stopped reading this because it was too hard.

• You quit brushing your teeth because your electric toothbrush was too difficult to operate.

• You decide not to watch television because you can't find the remote control – after looking for 20 seconds.

• Your idea of a workout is watching bowling on TV.

• You won't leave your bubble bath to urinate.

• You are unemployed, broke, and still pay someone to mow your lawn.

• You have failed in repeated attempts to build a cooler inside your recliner – not because it was vexing of a project, but because you didn't feel like looking for a screwdriver.

• After you go to the bathroom, instead of pulling up your pants, you just leave them down.

• You won't take a lunch break because you don't feel like getting out of your chair.

• You owe VISA $15,000, haven't paid them in nearly a year, and you're still telling whoever knocks on your door to "Come in" because you don't feel like getting up.

• You consider going to the convenience store to get beer "a night on the town."

• The only physical exercise you get is when you throw a pillow at someone standing between you and the television.

• After throwing the pillow, you decide it would take too much effort to go pick it up.

• After throwing the pillow, and deciding it would take too much effort to pick it up, you take off your shirt and use it as your pillow.

Do I have any comrades in laziness? Call me and let me know. Leave a message.

I'm not getting up to answer the phone.

I knows English,
but not defrosting car windows
April 4, 2001

My education has failed me.

Sure, I knows English.

And besides my inability to subtract, divide or multiply, I am a math whiz.

Science was never my bag, but I do remember that $E = MC$ squared is what most uneducated savages commonly call "water."

I was somewhat of a History prodigy, and have an instant recall of facts and dates from the Battle of Chateau Elan to the Salty II agreement.

As shown, the failure of my education didn't occur in what was taught in the classroom – it's in what I wasn't taught.

I was formally educated for 16 years and nowhere – not in one class, not by one teacher – was it ever mentioned how to properly defrost a car window.

In the years hence, this failure of the educational system has caused great strife in my life and literally seven or eight other people who are driving around and can't see a thing.

It would seem rather simple. If it's cold outside and your windows start fogging up, common sense tells you that it's hot on the inside, so you should turn your defrost on cold. Inversely, if it's hot outside and you're eating an Eskimo pie, making the inside of the vehicle very cold, then you should put the defrost on hot in order to see the road clearly.

But that's the enigma that is the riddle of defrosting your car window.

It doesn't always work the way common sense would dictate.

What usually happens on a cold morning is that you turn on the heat, and then your windows start fogging up. Being cold is no fun, so you turn the defrost on cold and your windows clear up for an instant. But then your teeth start chattering – a subtle sign you're cold again. You turn on the defrost, and the wicked cycle goes on forever.

Why even have a heater if you can't use it when it's cold?

Hot days are even more frustrating. Sometimes, a hot defrost will clear up your window on a sultry afternoon; sometimes a cold defrost will. By the time you figure out which, you're where you were going anyway. And the next time you get in the car, the routine you memorized mysteriously doesn't work again.

I find it extremely disturbing that our science community has found a way to clone sheep and change your hair color, but can't take the time to perfect a simple formula for the proper way to defrost a car window.

And if there is a formula that they are concealing, they need to reveal it and teach it in our schools. While reading, writing and arithmetic are indeed important, life skills like learning how to defrost your window are critical to everyone – from the Rhodes scholar to the road worker. I find it appalling that I learned the scientific formula for screwing in a lightbulb, "lefty-loosy, righty-tighty," not in my science class – where it should be a part of the curriculum – but from a movie (the underrated "Fandango").

While we're considering educational reforms in this country, why not add to the curricula the proper way to screw a lightbulb or how to clean a fish, or for the sake of safety and sanity everywhere, how to defrost a car window?

If not, don't blame me. When I tag your bumper while peering through a thick mist on my windshield, I have an excuse. I wasn't taught any better.

Going into the night like a wet rat?
From April 11, 2001

"Our Lord is a forgiving Lord."

That's how Sammy's eulogy began.

I'm no expert on eulogies. I've heard about a dozen or so, and, thankfully, haven't had to be the subject of one. But when a eulogy begins "Our Lord is a forgiving Lord," my thinking is that it's a good thing the eulogized isn't around to hear it. Because if he was, he would realize he was in for some serious reckoning.

My wife and father-in-law tell the story of their cousin Sammy's funeral, held many years ago at a Valdosta cemetery.

Sammy had lived a hard life, with his chief accomplishment being that he was an expert lock- and safe-cracker. On his coffin, there was a tiny lock holding Sammy's lid down.

"Sammy would crack that little thing in about half a second," my father-in-law whispered to my wife as the pastor rambled.

Of all a pastor's duties, I respect the eulogy the most. To have to come up with something to say – something that will soothe pain and put things in perspective, something that will capsulize a person's life – seems tremendously difficult, even when the deceased is a very popular, forthright person.

But think about the person the pastor didn't know too well. Or who strayed from God's path quite often. Or someone who always seemed down on their luck.

I guess you could just bury yourself in scripture, like Sammy's preacher did. Or you could start telling jokes. Or you could give someone else's eulogy. Sounds like a tough gig to me.

Toward the end of Sammy's eulogy, the pastor went in another direction – a bizarre one.

In closing, he said, "Sammy goeth into the night like a wet rat..."

I have no idea what he said after that. My wife and father-in-law were so flabberghasted by the "wet rat" reference, they paid little attention to the last few words.

"Did he just say 'wet rat?'"

Yes, they concurred. He said "wet rat." But what was the significance of the "wet rat?" Was it an analogy? A simile? A slip of the tongue? Was he meaning to say "Sammy goeth into the night like a wet nap?"

A wet cap? A ret wat?

We've called in biblical scholars, presenting them with the "goeth into the night like a wet rat." They're flummoxed.

Goeth into the night like a wet rat? I told you it was a tough gig.

Scantily-clad Mandrell Sisters write book about candy

May 2, 2001

When I was in high school, I was assigned to read one of the literary "classics" and deliver a report on it.

I chose "Grapes of Wrath."

A month later, I finished reading the book. I felt snookered even though I made a C.

The title, "Grapes of Wrath", is misleading. I wanted to read a book about grapes – angry grapes at that. What I found was that "Grapes of Wrath" wasn't about angry grapes at all, but rather about a bunch of people doing something that I can't remember.

All I wanted to do was read a book about grapes. What I uncovered in the process was the literary establishment's devious little secret.

What I found was the following: The publishing industry has been bamboozling the general public for years – titling books one thing, then having the text of the book be about something entirely different.

On subsequent assignments throughout my education, almost half of which were actually completed, I found this fraud to be the rule, not the exception.

My evidence:

• "Catcher in the Rye" is not a sports book about a catcher. Rather, it's about a young rich guy named Holden who doesn't even play baseball.

• "Little Women" isn't about female midgets working at a carnival or even the Mandrell Sisters. It's about women alright, but the author is rather vague about just how little they are.

• Bird hunters will be disappointed in "To Kill a Mockingbird," which is about justice and stuff.

• I enjoyed Pat Conroy's "Prince of Tides," but there's no prince in it, and very little reference to the tides.

• "Breakfast of Champions," by Kurt Vonnegut, is one of my favorite books, but I happened upon it looking for an easy novel to read. I figured, "How hard can a book about cereal be?" Nary a Fruity Pebble in the whole book.

• Folks wanting a good read about a candy bar (and who doesn't) will be foolhardy to check out "Looking for Mr. Goodbar." It's not the light-hearted romp about the search for a decent chocolatey snack I thought it was. Not even close. On the same note, "Marathon Man" isn't about a guy who loves Marathon bars.

Aren't there any good books about candy anymore?

- Even non-fiction books follow the industry's hoodwinking formula. "Men Are From Mars, Women Are From Venus" was a smash success by luring "Star Trek" geeks in with its sci-fi title. I read some of it, although I skipped the parts where it told men what to do. And gardening buffs made "Midnight in the Garden of Good and Evil" a bestseller by accident.

Mark Twain may be the only author who hasn't let the industry stain his titles. What's "The Adventures of Huckleberry Finn" about? The adventures of Huckleberry Finn, God bless America. What's "Life on the Mississippi" about? Why, it's about life on the Mississippi.

I'm going to follow suit. My first book, which is approximately 0 percent complete, will be titled "The Greatest Book Ever Written About Cheese." And it won't be about how eating ice cream makes my shoulder hurts (it does), or the Spanish-American War. It will be about cheese. I've added the mini-review in the title to clarify matters further.

I won't be a part of the conspiracy – unless, of course, I'm actually published.

Dodgeball banned! Next up: Mom, apple pie & Mr. Rogers

May 9, 2001

What in the (you fill it in) is the world coming to?

According to an absolutely real *New York Times* article, there is a nationwide effort to ban dodgeball – yes, the devilish dodgeball – from the nation's playgrounds.

Many of you may remember dodgeball from physical education classes of your youth. In the game, a group of players stand in between other players, throwing an oversized red ball at each other in a contest of elimination. The last player to avoid being hit wins.

Innocent enough, huh?

Well, not according to some folks.

"This (dodgeball) is something that should not be used in today's classroom, especially in today's society," Austin, Texas, curriculum specialist Diane Farr said in the story. Farr's district was the first in the nation to ban dodgeball. School districts in Virginia, Florida, New York, Massachusetts and Maine have followed suit.

"With Columbine and all the violence we are having, we have to be very careful with how we teach our children," Farr added, making no sense whatsoever. "What we have seen is that it (dodgeball) does not make students feel good about themselves."

Well, I didn't feel too good about myself when I made a D in Science either, but I didn't hear of an ensuing nationwide effort to ban the subject.

On this topic, let me be very subtle in expressing my opinion: This is stupid!

According to the story, Farr and her other Farr-out brethren contend that smaller children are often targets in dodgeball, and are apt to get injured.

I'm no scientist, as my D can attest, but isn't a smaller target harder to hit? In darts, do you get more points by hitting the wall or an innocent bystander or by hitting the much smaller bullseye?

I am a child of dodgeball. As the smallest kid in my first-, second-, third-, fourth-, fifth-, sixth-, seventh-, eighth-, and ninth-grade classes, dodgeball was my athletic oasis, where my lack of stature actually proved beneficially. I was so short and skinny nobody could hit me. I was always the winner, known to my schoolmates as "Mr. Dodgeball" (except for in first- and second-grades, when I was better known as "Len Pants-Falling-Down"). I was thinking of going pro, but a growth spurt at 14 ruined my chances of dodgeball superstardom.

Amazingly enough, even though I was burned many a time by that big red ball, I haven't shot anybody or committed any horrible acts of violence.

What exactly is this "connection" between dodgeball and school shootings? If we as a society are looking for knee-jerk reactions, why dodgeball? Why not something just as prone to cause school violence – like skipping or whistling? How about Mom and apple pie? And that Mr. Rogers – by acting nice, he could incite acting bad. Let's ban him too.

Methinks we need more kids being beaned in the noggin by dodgeballs – not less.

Long live dodgeball!

Common sense is already dead.

What she doesn't eat, I do – unfortunately
May 19, 2001

The two-year-old won't eat anything. The 32-year-old eats everything.

So goes in our household, where our daughter won't eat a thing we place directly in front of her, while her father gobbles down everything placed within a quarter-mile radius.

We should all eat like my daughter. She eats when she's hungry – scheduled meals be darned. Her old man eats whenever there is a scheduled meal, whenever there's not a scheduled meal, whenever he's hungry, whenever he's not hungry, whenever he's bored, whenever he's nervous, and whenever he's taking a shower.

Somehow, one small grape can propel an entire afternoon of running around our couch incessantly for her, but I need a double cheeseburger, the super-duper large fries, a 32-ounce Coke, and a light snack of Funyuns, jelly beans and a chocolate cake just to muster enough effort to get off the aforementioned couch to answer the phone.

While our daughter is rather small for her age, her doctor tells us she's in perfect health. Still, we've attempted all sorts of devious, and perhaps illegal, tactics to prompt more eating. We've begged. We've pleaded. We've cajoled. We've ordered. We've intimidated. We've played food games. We've tried the old "look over there" trick while we attempted to shove a banana in her mouth.

What we've realized is that, unlike her paunchy papa, this child eats when the urge hits her. As she gets older, we're told that she'll develop more of an appetite. We were also told that her father's eating habits were much like hers at that age.

Our child's loving relatives, though, don't want to wait for that eventuality. They want her to eat now!

On a recent trip to her great-grandmother's in Moultrie, our daughter was bombarded with offers of food from the moment she hit the door until the moment she left.

During one instance, her great-grandmother had prepared some link sausage. She arranged the two-inch-long, very brown links on a small plate and presented them to our daughter while she sat at the dinner table.

Our daughter looked down at the links of sausage, looked up at her great-grandmother with a puzzled look on her face, and in a quizzical tone, said "Poo-poo?"

As in, "you're serving me poo-poo?"

Ever since then, when she does decide to eat, she gives the thrice over to whatever meal we've placed before her, leery that we've snuck in some wretched refuse.

Oh, by the way, I ate the sausage links – just to make sure.

Strangely enough, my daughter doesn't want to kiss Daddy anymore.

A public thank you from me to you
May 23, 2001

Every week in this newspaper, "thank you" notes are printed by individuals or groups wanting to express their public appreciation. I think that's wonderful.

Too often, we forget to thank those who have helped us or done something outstanding to our benefit.

With that in mind, I have created my own public "thank you" note to show my appreciation to those who have, in some way, helped me over the years.

• First, I would like to publicly thank my parents for creating me. I'm no scientist, but I'm of the opinion that without their assistance, I probably wouldn't be here today.

I would also like to thank all the other individuals who helped raise me – step-parents, grandparents, aunts and uncles, my wife, my child, friends of the family, day-care providers, teachers, coaches, camp counselors, bus drivers, parole officers, wardens and court-appointed psychiatrists, and, of course, my attorney – all of you assisted in making me the gloriously humble person I am today.

• I would like to publicly thank my employers.

Despite my Gilliganesque antics and propensity to sleep while writing stories, they continue to pay me. For that, I, and my new 19-inch color television set, thank them.

• I would like to publicly thank the makers of Doritos.

Your yummy product has made many a cloudy day sunny to my stomach. I would also like to thank you for consorting with the french fry people to make me a lard-butt.

• I would like to publicly thank the VISA corporation for luring me into the wonderful world of credit cards.

You have taught me a valuable lesson about money – it's not free. Recently, I have converted to the Muslim faith and have abandoned my Christian moniker of Len Robbins. My new Muslim name is Larry "Dutch" Jenkins. All future VISA billing, correspondence and harassments should be delivered to that name.

• I would like to publicly thank Officer Gipson of the Athens Police Department.

Back when I was in college, Officer Gipson talked me out of going to class naked one day. In hindsight, I see that he was correct. That would have been a mistake. Again, I would like to thank my attorney for his representation in that matter.

• I would like to publicly thank Sir Isaac Newton.

Unlike Sir Mix-a-Lot, Sir Isaac Newton earned his knighthood. While everyone recognizes Sir Newton as the inventor of Fig Newtons, it is a little known fact that he also invented gravity (with just a kite and a key, no less!)

Because of his ingenuity, I understand what law of physics applies when I drop one of his fruity treats.

• Finally, I'd like to publicly thank anyone who has ever forgiven me, or not, for anything I ever did, or didn't do, to them.

I'd also like to thank in advance anyone that I ever offend, slight, publicly humiliate or accidently maim in the future for their understanding and forgiving nature. And, of course, I'd like to thank my attorney for his future kindness in bailing me out of jail and taking my money. It is because of people like you, and my attorney, that I am who I am today, and tomorrow.

With that in mind, give yourself a big thank you. You deserve it.

You may live in a small town when...

May 30, 2001

Living in a small town has its advantages and shortcomings.

I tend to think graduating from high school with the policeman that pulls you over for speeding is more beneficial than getting a decent taco.

With this in mind, I have compiled the following list – most of which I've actually seen or had happen to me while living in a small town. With apologies to Jeff Foxworthy, you may live in a small town when:

• Half of the jury pool has to be excused because they are related to the defendant.

• The Sheriff's Department dispatcher makes wake-up calls.

• You know the town Peeping Tom by his first name.

• In a 20-yard area, you see more than three people with a t-shirt or hat that says "You Can Have My Gun When You Pry It From My Cold, Dead Hands" – in church.

• A father and son get in a car accident – with each other, six miles from their home.

• The guy paving your driveway puts "police tape" up after he completes the job, and 30 minutes later, somebody from your church shows up at your door with a bunt cake and a plate of fried chicken as a show of condolence.

• Crazy people are merely considered "eccentric."

• You receive a call from someone who found your wallet at a basketball game. He tells you to pick it up at the jail because that's where he's staying – as a prisoner.

• A substitute mail carrier can turn the whole town upside down.

• You are a pallbearer in three funerals in a week.

• The power company calls to warn you they are about to turn your power off.

• There are people who still just have a conventional phone – no call waiting, no answering machine, no cell phone.

• You know all the dogs in town by their name.

• There are still establishments where you can "charge" merchandise, or they operate by the "honor system."

• The same minister that married you also put the roof on your house.

• Businesses close down when a prominent community member dies.

• A stranger can get directions to anybody in town's house at a convenience store.

• The stranger gets those directions in the form of "you turn right at the old Johnson homeplace, then go about 100 yards and turn left where Marvin Brewer grew up, and their house is just past that on the right. A blue Impala will be in the front yard. But don't get out, because that dog will bite you."

They also know the name of that dog.

I pledge allegiance to all the butterflies...
June 25, 2001

"Amen" was easy.

What goes before that has been tricky.

They say old habits die hard. With that in mind, we are attempting to instill some good habits in our young daughter that we hope will die old. Blessings and prayers are currently on our two-year-old's plate.

While she has grasped the "Amen" part with enthusiastic gusto, she tends to deviate from the script with the prelude.

Sometimes, when we ask her to say a blessing before a meal, she puts her little hands together and delivers it perfectly.

Other times, well...

"God is great. God is good. Let us thank him for our... hands. A-men!"

Her night-time prayers follow the same pattern, as she is prone to free-flowing, corner-cutting improvisation.

"As I lay me down to sleep, I pray the Lord...for morning light. A-men!"

A while back, we began an addendum to her memorized prayer, where she asks God to bless her grandparents, or friends, or daycare providers, or whoever her heart tells her. Sometimes, her heart is in her stomach.

"God bless...umm, cookies and Pop-Tarts. A-men!"

Other times, whatever is on her mind at that moment is the subject of her prayers.

"God bless the lady who was crying on TV...and all the butterflies. A-men!"

I think the lady who was crying was on a dandruff commercial.

Of course, she's only two. And memorization can be trying business – even for adults.

I remember a former colleague of mine in Tifton who once had to fill in for a fellow sportswriter covering a Tift County High baseball game. When he got to the stadium, he was informed that the sportswriter he was filling in for also doubled as the public address announcer. He really had no choice but to adopt that duty as well.

Right before the game started, he was instructed to ask everybody to stand and lead them over the P.A. system in reciting the Pledge of Allegiance. He did as he was told – sort of.

"Everyone please stand for the Pledge of Allegiance," he said solemnly and deeply into the microphone as all the players and the hundreds of spectators at the game stood and stared reverently at the flag waving in centerfield.

Then he started: "I pledge allegiance to the flag of the United States of America...thy Kingdom come, thy will be done, on earth as it is in Heaven. Give us this day our daily bread, and forgive us for our trespasses, as we forgive those who trespass against us. Lead us not into temptation, but deliver us from evil. For thine is the Kingdom and the power and the glory, forever and ever. Amen."

Whether you're two or 32 – I guess it doesn't really matter how it comes out, or even if you end up with a pledge/Lord's Prayer hybrid. God knows what you're saying.

A-men!

Twenty good reasons to stay in bed this morning
August 22, 2001

I've decided on my epitaph.

It will say: "He did say he loved to sleep."

That, or: "Whatchu talkin' about Willis?"

There are some mornings I just don't feel like getting up. Not really that many – only about 365 annually. If I'm not awake, I'd rather be sleeping. Or eating Doritos. Or watching football on television. I tried doing all three simultaneously back in '93 and ended up in the hospital, but that's something I'm not really comfortable talking about.

When that snooze alarm goes off, I sometimes get up. Later, I regret that rash decision. To combat that daily feeling of sorrow and rue, I have come up with 20 sort-of legitimate reasons not to get up in the morning. As a public service, I am passing off these sleepy pearls of wisdom to you, the reader. You can use them as excuses for your boss when you're late to work. Or you can do as I have – post them next to your alarm, and when it tolls for your arousal in the morn, simply consult the list and go back to the land of Nod satisfied that you have made a wise, informed, thoughtless choice.

Here are your 20 good reasons not to get up this morning:

1. You can't possibly get everything done today you're supposed to.
2. You could get stung by a bee.
3. Picking out underwear is much too taxing.
4. It's just going to be night again in about 16 hours or so.
5. Today could be the day that year 2000 computer stuff hits the fan.
6. You have the rest of your life to work.
7. You need more time sleeping to see if you are snoring too loud.
8. The Queen of England doesn't have to get up and work. Why should you?
9. A meteor could be crashing to Earth right now. Do you really want to be outside?
10. They don't sell beer at work.
11. Why you? Can't someone else get up and do your job? Sure they can.
12. You could catch cooties.
13. It's too hot.
14. It's too cold.

15. It's absolutely perfect weather, but you forgot where all your clothes are.

16. That episode of "Facts of Life" you missed in 1984 is supposed to be on the USA network at 11:30 a.m. You don't want to miss that again.

17. Today could be the day a bird finally nails you.

18. Although you haven't read your horoscope, it could say something bad is going to happen to you today.

19. Your car probably won't start anyway.

20. You work eight hours and sleep eight hours. Shouldn't it be the other way around?

Happy snoozing!

Bad-mouth America? Here's the facts, Jack

September 26, 2001

*"I, for one, am not going to sit here and watch you bad-mouth the
United States of America!"*

> – Otter,
> "Animal House"

Some of our brethren on this earth are talking about us.

If you're like me, you're currently wearing pants, and you've
also been watching the television news programs and scouring the
newspapers over the last few weeks for reasons other than college
football scores.

What I've learned is that not every person in this world loves the
good ole U.S. of A. Some are saying we Americans are arrogant. We're
overbearing. We're spoiled. Us!

Obviously, they don't know what the heck they're talking about.
I am about to learn them.

Below are just a few of the millions of reasons earthlings worldwide
should love and appreciate the red, white and blue of the United States
of America.

• Elvis was born here.

Have you noticed they always describe some singer as the "Elvis of
Albania" but never, ever have I heard anyone refer to Elvis Presley as
the "Karstimuhl of America."

• We invented Doritos.

• We, predominantly, saved the world from the Nazis.

France, for one, can't seem to remember that.

• Our country is the only one in the world where someone with no
discernible talent whatsoever like Ed McMahon or Pauly Shore can
become a celebrity.

• Every few years, we produce some wacky fad like bell bottoms or
disco or electricity or the steam engine or the automobile that sweeps
the world.

• Millions of people flock to stadiums every Saturday here to watch
college football games.

• We'll give a standing ovation to our president every few seconds
just for speaking.

- "The Andy Griffith Show" was written, produced and filmed right here in America.
- Missionaries from our country are currently in every corner of the globe, trying to make life better for others.
- I was in Wal-mart last week watching TV when the race commentator said someone was from New Mexico. The guy standing next to me said, "What? There's a new Mexico? What happened to the old one?" That man is probably allowed to vote here.
- We make the best barbecue of any place on earth.
- We also have Spam.
- We welcome everybody in the world to become an American.
- We have convenience stores here where you can buy a $4 hat that says "My Wife Ran Off With My Best Friend and I Miss Him."
- There are pockets of our country where cars pull to the side of the road for a funeral procession.
- Some of us cry when "God Bless America" is played or when we watch the end of "Revenge of the Nerds."
(Note: That may just be me)
- No matter who your parents are, how rich or poor you are, or what race, ethnic group or religious denomination you belong to, you are allowed to achieve success here.
- Almost everybody who ever came to this country had nothing.
Arrogant? Overbearing? Spoiled? No, no and maybe.

The truth is this: We're proud of who we are, and how we got to where we are, and we should be. The truth is also this: Most of this international grumbling about our country, and the root of those who hate us, is jealousy.

We also call it like we see it.

Napping the key to workplace prosperity
January 23, 2002

As a small businessman (5-foot-9), I'm always on the lookout for ways to improve productivity and employee morale.

Over the years, some of my workplace improvement ideas have worked splendidly – 'Popsicle Wednesday' being a great example. Some haven't fared as well – the ill-fated "Monday Morning Sing-A-Longs" escalating into ugliness.

But this time, I think I am on to something that will revolutionize the American workforce, making our laborers happier, more productive, cure scurvy, inspire some new hymns, and perhaps end the Cold War.

I can't speak for other businesses, but the greatest impediment to workplace productivity and joy in the world is what I have termed the "Mid-Day Slump." Around 2-3 p.m. each day, employees everywhere, myself included, find themselves in the throes of a tired and uninspired malaise. Efficiency and morale drops. Nothing gets done. Tempers flare at the drop of a paper clip.

Around here, I see this "Mid-Day Slump" manifest itself daily in behaviors that could be considered non-profitable and adverse to good customer service, such as screaming at customers, drooling on computer terminals, and battles over the thermostat that end with staplers being used as weapons of minor destruction.

For years, I've sought a cure to this workplace ailment – none successful (employees don't like you when you attempt to wake them up using a cattle prod). Last week, my three-year-old daughter gave me the nudging I needed to invent my startling breakthrough.

She told me that every day after lunch, she is forced to take a nap.

It's that simple – a nap. Think about it in these terms: Every Sunday, I take a nap around 2 p.m. When I wake up, at about 6:30 p.m., I am refreshed, renewed, and eager to tackle all sorts of projects, like watching the end of the football game.

She said a nap recharges her batteries for the rest of the day and diminishes the possibility of screaming, hair-pulling, drooling, and/or stapler-heaving episodes.

After her rejuvenating snooze, she has the vigor to spend the rest of her day happily jumping about, sticking things in other kids' mouths, and yelling for no apparent reason.

Just think of the productivity adult workplaces could achieve if workers had the energy in the afternoons to jump about, stick things in other employees' mouths, and yell for no apparent reason for hours.

Upon further research, I've found that Europe has had a different version of my idea in place for centuries. In Italy, workers break up the workday by having a long lunch, where they consume too much wine, then take a nap. This schedule has done wonders for their prosperity, as they've risen from the dark days of the Roman Empire to their current status as an international economic non-entity.

In Spain (it's a country in Europe too – I think?), they also take a mid-day slumber. They call it a "siesta." So as not to confuse us Americans, we'll simply call it "Len Robbins' Mid-Day American Workers' Nap."

Happy dozing!

And businesses – let the good times roll!

Baseball on strike? I offer my services

May 22, 2002

Bud Selig
Commissioner
Major League Baseball

Dear Mr. Selig:

Recently, while perusing a copy of *Mad* magazine, I saw a cartoon indicating that major league baseball players may go on strike soon.

If a strike does indeed come to fruition, I am offering my services to major league baseball as a replacement player. I have spoken to my family about this scenario and the sacrifices they will have to make.

I'll be honest – they weren't too thrilled about the prospect of me being away a couple of weeks a year during the long major league baseball season. But then I told them: "Being a professional baseball player will allow us to have all the things we have always dreamed of – A big house, lots of fancy cars, our own entourage of hangers-on and ne'er-do-well high school buddies that don't have jobs, cable service every day of the month, a dozen or so pet chimpanzees, a waterfall in the living room, some of those Ginsu knives, a go-cart, and all the pork rinds we can eat." After that, they were all for it. In fact, they forced me to leave immediately. I'm currently living in an abandoned van behind my cousin's house until I get the call from "The Bigs."

For your consideration are some of the highlights of my baseball career:

1974 – Yankees t-ball team. Earned raves from my 15-year-old coach, Steve, who called me a "hardly mediocre" third baseman. Led my team to an undefeated record. Due to a unprecedented mathematical enigma, did not receive a championship ring (or a lousy parade for that matter) because every team in the league held an undefeated record.

1975-1987 – Like Roy Hobbs of "The Natural," I left the game under mysterious circumstances. Don't want to dish the dirty details, but I cut my catching hand in a freak tuna can opening incident, and it hurt really bad.

1987 – Like Roy Hobbs of "The Natural," I mysteriously re-entered the baseball arena. Actually, it was softball (sort of like baseball, only softer). I was a lightning-slow rightfielder for the Myers Hall Second-

Floor Gastros. First on the team in walks, hit-by-pitches and getting-caught-in-rundowns. Led team to sterling 4-7 record, losing coin flip for playoff spot to loaded Rutherford Hall Lady Braves team.

1988-1990 – Unlike Roy Hobbs of "The Natural," I was thrown off the Gastros the next season by the manager (whom I only knew as "Bromo") after my participation in shaving his eyebrows off after he had passed out drunk.

2000-2002 – Like Roy Hobbs again, I mysteriously re-emerged a decade later, playing coed church softball. Just recently, I went 1-for-3 in a game, robbed of hits on two scorching dribblers by a Brooks Robinson-like middle-aged lady at third.

In addition to my impressive t-ball, college and church league credentials, I also have this to offer:

• I'll play cheap. I'll take a salary of $100,000 for the whole season, or $200,000 a base hit, whichever comes first.

• When I'm not in the field, I'd also like to offer my services as side-show entertainment, sort of like a mascot with a uniform. I have considerable experience at crowd-pleasing antics like pulling down umpires' pants, taking foul balls away from elementary-school kids, and tackling beer vendors. No matter how many touchdowns we trail by, with me on the team, the fans are going to be entertained.

• I am a master heckler and dugout chatter-box. I do a mean "swa-wing, batta, batta, batta, swa-wing batta!" I'm also quite adept at ad-libbing insulting limericks, usually focusing on the opposing batter's mother.

Mr. Selig, what I lack in batting, fielding, throwing, running, catching, baseball knowledge, ability to tell the truth, hot-footing prowess (I tend to set the whole person on fire), and overall character, I make up for with moxie, hustle, gusto, showmanship, other good stuff, and having absolutely no fear of making a fool of myself for money.

I look forward to my new career in major league baseball and hearing from you soon.

Go Brewers!
Len Robbins

P.S. If you could, please place me on either the Atlanta Braves or that team Roy Hobbs played for, the New York Knights. I'd love to play for that legendary baseball manager, Wilford Brimley.

'Daddy's Mobile Day Care' hits the road
June 5, 2002

Many a classic book or film has used the device of a journey or "road trip" to weave a tale, theme or moral. "Grapes of Wrath," "The Adventures of Huckleberry Finn," "The Odyssey," "National Lampoon's Vacation," and "Pee Wee's Big Adventure," are just a few that come immediately to mind, and the list goes on and on.

Add "Daddy's Mobile Day Care" to that list.

Memorial Day weekend, a family outing was planned in Athens. My wife was to be there already for a work-related function, meaning I had to cart our three-year-old daughter and five-month-old son by my lonesome to Athens. Below is the blow-by-blow account of what usually is a four-hour trek:

Friday, noon – Estimated time of departure.

Friday, 12:50 p.m. – Actual time of departure. Van packed to the rims with toys, clothes, wipes, candy, and none of the items on the list my wife told me to bring. Kids secure in their car seats. Have already made arrangements for their optimum drowsiness: Told the day care to withhold my daughter's mid-afternoon nap; gave my son a dose of Benadryl, chased with a shot of Dickel.

1:15 p.m. – "Daddy, I've got to tee-tee," makes its first appearance.

1:20 p.m. – After a debate on the level of "tee-tee" urgency, stop at the Hardee's in Pearson, where I have to walk my daughter to the men's room with my son in the car seat – not an easy task, I assure you.

1:32 p.m. – "Daddy, I'm hungry," makes its first appearance.

1:41 p.m. – Stop at the Wendy's in Douglas to secure food for my starving daughter. Unfortunately, they aren't serving her requested pancakes at 1:41 p.m. She settles for french fries, I get a frosty, and we're off. I end up eating her discarded french fries somewhere around Jacksonville, Georgia.

2:22 p.m. – Daughter finally sacks out, son hasn't been heard from since we left home (he's a lightweight), and I'm caught in radio's Bermuda Triangle. Forced to resort to AM, searching for ESPN radio to no avail.

2:50 p.m. – Reach Dublin, where the solace abruptly ends. Son begins to scream, then stops, then screams a little more. Daughter wakes up, picks up the "tee-tee" refrain, coupled with the addendum of "I scream, you scream, we all scream for ice cream!"

3:02 p.m. – Pull into the Piggly Wiggly parking lot. Go to the back of the van to feed my son, and let my daughter out of her car seat to roam about freely. This proves to be a mistake, as she finds some scissors and begins to cut everything in sight – her coloring book, the newspaper, proof of insurance, my checkbook.

3:25 p.m. – Finally get back on the road.

3:27 p.m. – Get off the road to "tee-tee" and search for ice cream at a convenience store. After towing the whole clan into the restroom (where my daughter kept asking for a quarter to get the prize off the bathroom wall), we can't find any ice cream to our liking (actually, her liking) and trudge back to the van and onto 441.

4:01 p.m. – Just when I find ESPN radio, my daughter decides she's in a chatty mood. My attention is torn between the latest sports news and my daughter's ramblings until I hear her say: "I'm going to Dr. Sam to have the cabbage removed from my foot." After a lengthy interrogation, I determine that she was mimicking something she heard an adult say, replacing "cabbage" for "corn."

4:37 p.m. – My son, relatively quiet the entire trip, discovers something new about himself. He can make very loud noises. This makes him quite happy.

5:04 p.m. – Just before Madison, five hours of being strapped to a chair inside of a van manifests itself in a dizzying display of screaming, crying and hissy fits – and the kids were sort of grumpy too.

We stop at another convenience store to peruse the bathrooms and assortment of ice cream. While purchasing some gum from a young, thoroughly-pierced clerk, my daughter offers: "Daddy, that girl has a shiny booger in her nose." I sheepishly apologize, and then chortle to myself as soon as we're out of earshot.

5:34 p.m. – Finally leave the convenience store, bound and determined to not make another pit stop for the rest of the allotted 30-minute journey. We don't, although my son had clearly had enough (possibly a hangover).

6:04 p.m. – Arrive at our destination, my sister's house in Athens. Mom wraps the kids in hugs as soon as we stop rolling. A crowbar is used to pry Daddy's hands from steering wheel.

I have a new-found respect for Clark Griswald.

You may live in a small town when... Part II
June 12, 2002

Last year about this time, I wrote a column entitled, "You may live in a small town when..."

The headline gave it away. The column listed things that may indicate you live in a small town. Since then, I have been besieged by literally one or two people with more ideas on this topic. Following my philosophy of avoiding original material (makes my head hurt), I have rounded up some of these suggestions and added a few of my own – most of which I've actually seen or had happen to me.

Again, with apologies to Jeff Foxworthy, you may live in a small town when:

• In the Sunday morning announcements at your church, the minister says, "The Good-Timers are going to Alma Thursday to eat at Hillbillies Restaurant."

• You receive and send mail with just the person's name and hometown on the envelope.

• There's an undertaker in your town who has a "side" occupation (In Mayberry, he doubled as a TV repairman. In Summerville, Ga., he sells barbecue – from the same building).

• Parent-teacher conferences are conducted on Aisle 4 at the local grocery store.

• Your neighbor has a cow in his front yard tied to a leash – and there's nothing you can do about it; nor do you care.

• The police call you at a wedding rehearsal dinner to tell you your front door is unlocked.

• You have at least two nicknames that stick with you your entire life – one family nickname (examples-"Bubba," "Sissy," "Bebe," "Young 'un") and one high school nickname (examples-"Frostbite," "Hellrat," "Boogie Night," "Bacon Strip").

• You skip school for 10 minutes to get a bite to eat and somebody from the community tells school officials before you get back.

• You ask somebody where they want to eat by saying, "Which one – Hardees or Dairy Queen?"

• UPS delivers a package to your home that's addressed to your work – or vice versa.

• You've called a pharmacist at home on Sunday to order a prescription.

• People in your town are offended if you don't have some type of NASCAR-related paraphernalia on your vehicle.

• You've been "boggin" before.

• Your monthly tab at the local flower shop is more than your power bill.

• You are on trial for a crime and four members of the jury taught you – and flunked you – in high school.

Hasn't happened to me (yet), but I've seen it happen.

Sequels are never as good as the original.

Parenting lessons from Mayberry

July 10, 2002

A number of years ago, I wrote a column focusing on "The Andy Griffith Show" that somehow ended up at the bottom of Jim Clark's birdcage.

Clark is the president (official title – "Head Goober") of The Andy Griffith Show Rerun Watchers Club (TAGSRWC). Clark was kind enough to send me an honorary subscription to his club's newsletter, *The Bullet,* and other information on the club's events.

Recently, I received in the mail a copy of Clark's new book, *Act Like Somebody: Special Moments from The Andy Griffith Show,* written with Ken Beck. They also published a companion book, *I'm Proud to Call You My Friend: A Collection of Special Moments of Friendship from The Andy Griffith Show.*

As a semi-new parent, *Act Like Somebody* especially appealed to me, with brief synopses of parenting conundrums faced by Sheriff Andy Taylor and how he handled them. Below are some that stood out to me, and, maybe, to you:

• "Opie's Charity": Opie gives just three cents to the underprivileged children's charity, and Andy attempts to explain why Opie needs to give more.

Andy: "I was reading just the other day where there's somewhere like four hundred needy boys in this county alone. Or one and a half boys per every square mile."

Opie: "There is?"

Andy: "There sure is."

Opie: "I never seen one."

Andy: "Never seen one what?"

Opie: "A half a boy."

Andy: "Well, it's not really half a boy. It's a ratio."

Opie: "Horatio who?"

• "The Horse Traders": Opie has traded his new cap pistol for what turned out to be phony licorice seeds and now plans to trade the licorice seeds to another friend for roller skates. Andy tries to set his son straight.

Andy: "Let me tell you something here. You know that you've been taught the Golden Rule: Do unto others as you'd have them do unto you?"

Opie: "Yes, Pa."

Andy: "You think you've been following that rule?"

Opie: "Sure. Tommy did unto me and now I'm doing unto Jerry."

• "One-Punch Opie": After a new boy prompts Opie and some his friends into some mischief, Barney gives Andy some unsolicited advice on how to handle the situation.

Andy: "Barney, these are just boys we're talking about. They're only about eight years old."

Barney: "Yeah, well, today's eight-year-olds are tomorrow's teenagers. I say this calls for action – and now. Nip it in the bud! First sign of youngsters goin' wrong, you got to nip it in the bud."

Andy: "I'm gonna have a talk with 'em. Now, what more you want me to do?"

Barney: "Yeah, well, just don't mollycoddle 'em. Nip it! You go read any book you want on the subject of child discipline and you'll find that every one of 'em is in favor of bud nippin'."

• "Opie and the Spoiled Kid": Barney again pushes for stricter discipline when a spoiled kid influences Opie.

Barney: "There's a definite trend toward stronger discipline."

Andy: "Like what?"

Barney: "Like a good clout once in a while."

Andy: "Oh, come on."

Barney: "Well, Andy, have you ever known the magazine section of the Sunday paper to lie?"

Andy: "Did your father ever hit you?"

Barney: "Well, he couldn't. I was a lot bigger than he was."

• "Bailey's Bad Boy": (One of my personal favorites – saw it again just last week) Bill Bixby plays Ron Bailey, a young man in custody for reckless driving. He overhears Opie tell Andy that he broke Miss Purdy's window with a ball. Andy tells Opie he's going to have to pay for the window.

Ron: "Weren't you sorta rough on the kid?"

Andy: "How's that?"

Ron: "Well, why didn't you bail the little fella out?"

Andy: "Bail him out?"

Ron: "Well, yeah. It's just a window."

Andy: "Oh, oh, oh, oh, oh, oh. Yeah, yeah, I guess I could bail him out like you say. But the only trouble with that – if I was to do that, why, every time he'd get into trouble, he'd be expecting me to come to the rescue, don't you see. This time it's a broken window, later on it'd be something bigger, and then something bigger than that. No, he's got to learn to stand on his own two legs. No, I gotta keep that young 'un straight."

Who says we have nothing to learn from TV?

A pretend architect's trash-can solution
September 18, 2002

I'm no architect, although I've pretended to be one at a couple of class reunions.

But if I were an architect, my first order of business would be to design some homes where you can find a trash can.

Why is it that people want to hide their trash cans? Do they believe that if we can't find their trash can, we won't think they produce garbage?

I hate to burst anyone's bubble, but every home produces wretched refuse – even the Queen of England's (she has to discard of popsicle sticks too).

Back to my make-believe vocation as an architect. Here's what I would do: First, I would put a round, three-foot-wide, four-foot-tall brick garbage receptacle right in the middle of the kitchen – built into the floor like a massive grill. No more guests having to search through all of my cabinets to find the trash. It would be bricked in, right smack dab in the middle of the kitchen. If folks still didn't recognize it as the trash, I would put a big sign over it. That sign would say: "This is the trash. Loiter all you want. No fishing."

Built into my ingenuous idea are a couple of small hitches. Don't worry, I have them covered.

First, with a garbage can right in the middle of the kitchen, there might be the small potential for unappealing aromas. Folks that cook cabbage wouldn't be bothered, but others with more discernible olfactory senses could be. My solution: A lid.

Problem #2 is a little more complicated – what to do with the trash once it's in the bricked-in garbage can?

As much as I hate making the painful effort to search through peoples' cabinets for a trash can, I find it even more exhausting to actually take the garbage out of the can and transport it – by foot! – all the way to the bigger garbage can outside.

What I've found is that there are all these pipes under my house. Yours may have them too. If your home doesn't, you may want to look into getting some. Anyway, if I was an architect, and we're pretending I am, I would create a device to put at the bottom of my bricked-in garbage can that would squish the garbage and send it through those pipes. I would call this device "The Squisher."

The pipes would then transport the squished garbage out of my premises to wherever they go. Where do they go? I have no idea. But they would be out of my premises, which is all I, as a pretend architect, care about.

I guess I'll just have to wait for a real architect to steal my idea. In the meantime, I've given up on finding trash cans in homes where they insist on hiding them. My empty Dr Pepper bottle can be found under the plant next to the window.

I'm telemarketing's favorite customer

October 30, 2002

"Hello, is this Allen Robbins?"

When I answer the phone and hear that, the caller is one of two people: Mrs. Harris, my seventh-grade math teacher (the last person to regularly call me by my proper first name); or it's a telemarketer.

Since Mrs. Harris hated my guts, I assume it's a telemarketer and respond to their query with the following in the highest-pitched voice I can muster: "No, my daddy isn't here."

Of course, they always ask if "my mommy" is there. I tell them no. Then, they ask when my daddy will be home. I usually respond with "when he's paroled." That ends the conversation.

This scenario occurs about twice an evening, even though it's not supposed to happen at all. My wife signed us up for some "no-telemarketing" thing through the phone company. Didn't work.

Then, my in-laws, who have apparently been staying up way too late, and drinking lots of Colt .45 out of the can, bought me some device called "The Zapper" for my birthday. You're supposed to be able to hook up "The Zapper" to your phone and it "zaps" telemarketers – hence the name. I don't know if the zapping hurts them or not. All I know is that every time I answer the phone, I hear a click, which I assume is "The Zapper" at work.

While "The Zapper" doesn't work at all (I still get calls from telemarketers), the click does serve a purpose in that I often pretend like the click is my call waiting and can thus dodge unwanted conversations with non-telemarketers and telemarketers alike.

My problem with telemarketing calls is not that I consider them a huge nuisance. They are just doing their job. I know. For a couple of lowly months in college, I myself was a telemarketer, selling the aforementioned call waiting and other telephone services to unsuspecting people in New Jersey who didn't speak English. Or, at least they didn't understand my English. I never could get a response when I would ask, "How ya'll doin' d'day?"

No, the problem for me with telemarketers is that I'm a sucker.

I'll buy anything from anybody at any time for any price. And if they are Girl Scouts, or a church youth group, or blind, or veterans – or blind, veteran, church-going Girl Scouts – I'll buy three.

I have five years worth of irregular light bulbs that won't fit any socket in my house, a three-year subscription to *Cat Fancy* magazine, a two-year-old fruitcake the size of Peter O'Toole's liver (and mysteriously growing), and an air filtration system that I only use at night to lull me to sleep, as a testament to my utter susceptibility to the hoodwink of telemarketing.

Maybe that's how I got "The Zapper" in the first place.

Terrorists won't stop ketchup consumption
November 6, 2002

I had some french fries.

They were warm and I assumed they were yummy.

I needed some ketchup, the King of Condiments, to make them yummier (A sidenote: Catsup is the Sickly Prince of Condiments).

The ketchup was housed in one of those large squeeze bottles. I like those. Anything that hurries the process of ketchup consumption is a friend of mine.

I grabbed the ketchup bottle, juxtaposing it at a 75-degree angle northwest of my french fries. I squeezed. Nothing came out. I squeezed harder. Again, nothing. I squeezed a third time, this time grunting from my meager feat of strength. Nothing.

Oh, silly me, I forgot to open that little flip-top cap.

I tried again. No ketchup. Curses! I peered into the eye of the cap. There was something blocking the ketchup. I unscrewed the lid. Underneath the lid was a white seal over the top of the ketchup bottle. I thought about giving up. A little voice in my head said: "Len, remember what Jimmy Valvano said: 'Don't give up. Don't ever give up.'"

I was thusly motivated. I was pumped. I was concerned about a voice being in my head where the monkey on the wheel was supposed to be. But more than that, I was hungry – or rather, I wasn't full, which is what hunger is to me.

Plan A was then formed. I would peel the seal (he, he, that rhymed) off the top of the ketchup bottle. Plan A failed. I have no fingernails to speak of, making me defenseless in girl fights and/or battles to open ketchup bottles. I tried and tried with my nubby nails, but couldn't get a grip on the steely gateway to yumminess.

I spent the next five minutes formulating Plan B. Plan B, when finalized, included bashing the seal with my shoe. It failed.

Plan C followed. It involved a crowbar to no success. During the process of carrying out Plan D, I discovered that a person can suffer painful second-degree burns by holding a strong lighter upside down. Plan F taught me that an egg beater is good for absolutely nothing but beating eggs.

Around Plan J, I began to wonder why this indestructible little white cap was on my ketchup bottle in the first place. My mind wandered back to the 1980s, when some wacko was injecting cyanide into Tylenol products. After that, safety caps started appearing on everything. But since that point, 20 years later, we haven't had any widespread product tampering scares, much less assaults on ketchup bottles.

So why are we still doing it? Is it a national security issue? Is this where the terrorists will strike next? By contaminating the national ketchup supply? Oh, heavens no.

Plan N was messy, but it worked. The corkscrew penetrated the seal, allowing ketchup to slowly flow through the tattered seal and the nearly-destroyed cap. My french fries were no longer hot and crisp, but rather cold and soggy. The King of Condiments, though, did pep them up a little.

I will not let the terrorists win.

Directions are different in a small town

November 20, 2002

I was forced to go to Atlanta the other day.

Here were the directions I received to my destination: Take I-75 North to I-75/I-85. Then take I-85 North. Get off on exit 56 at Peachtree Dunwoody Road. Ten miles later, take a right at Peachtree Road. After 43 stop lights, take a right on Peachtree Lane. Fourteen stop lights later, take a left on Peachtree Terrace. After the mall, take a right on Peachtree Trace. Cross Peachtree Road again. Nine stop lights and three caution lights later, take a left on Peachtree Corners Lane.

Of course, being that no road in Atlanta is straight, I lost my usually-acute sense of direction and ended up paying some guy $14 to find my way.

He told me to get back on Peachtree.

Here are the directions newcomers need to find me in my small town: Stop at the convenience store. Ask the cashier where I am.

That's pretty much it.

True story: When I was a freshman in college, some guys who lived in my dorm were coming back from spring break in Florida when their car broke down in Homerville. They only knew me and my roommate, who was also from Homerville, by our first names. It was on Sunday. They were from Atlanta. They were scared to death.

After an hour or so of twiddling their thumbs, one of the stranded remembered that those two guys who lived in Room 268 were from a small town named Homerville.

On what they thought was a whim, they walked into a convenience store and asked the cashier, "do you know a guy from here named Len?"

The cashier replied with: "Yeah, but he's already gone back to school today. But Stan ain't left yet."

The cashier then called my roommate Stan, who was about to leave for Athens. Stan woke a mechanic up from his Sunday nap, got him to fix their car, and they were on their way.

But like the befuddled country bumpkin losing his way among the Peachtrees, it's also possible for the citified to be directionally stumped.

When my wife first moved to my hometown, a co-worker directed her somewhere by saying: "Go through the redlight, turn left where the old drive-in used to be, then turn right at the house where Jimmy Douglas grew up."

Where the old drive-in used to be? How was she supposed to find that?

One other advantage of getting directions in a small town: The cashier at the convenience store probably won't charge you for it.

But you probably should buy something – just to be polite.

10 little girls, 16 hours, 1 scared man
January 15, 2003

This past weekend, my wife invited nine girls ages 3-5 to our house for a spend-the-night party for our daughter's 4th birthday.

I have no idea why my wife would do such a thing – perhaps it is a condition of her probation.

Anyway, she had the whole thing organized to the finest detail. The girls would arrive at 6. They would dine on hot dogs, chips and pink lemonade. They would bake cookies. They would open presents. They would paint each other's toenails. They would load up in the den, get in their sleeping bags, and watch a movie until they fell asleep.

Her plan worked to perfection.

They arrived at 6 p.m. Friday. They ate, then baked cookies. We opened presents, then they dolled up and painted toenails. Then we laid out all the sleeping bags and told them to go to sleep.

Problem was – it was only 7:20.

We had gone through the whole night's agenda and we still had 14 hours and 40 minutes left.

"Maybe we shouldn't have told them to get here at 6 at night and leave at 10 in the morning," my wife admitted.

"Yeah, it should have been the other way around," I offered. "Arrive at 10 p.m., leave at 6 a.m."

I knew I was in for something new, different, and potentially horrifying as soon as the parents dropped off their children. As the parents exited out the back door, I witnessed most of them sprinting to their cars, laughing hysterically. I swear I heard one of them scream "Sucker!" Then, later, when any of them called to check on their children, they were at some restaurant out of town – living it up.

While we ran out of organized activities after an hour and a half, the girls filled the gaps.

Within seconds of their arrival, every one of them had changed from the color-coordinated outfit their parents had picked for them into some type of ballet dancer/cheerleader/majorette/street walker uniform.

They then proceeded to scream even the most common of phrases for the next two hours.

"Would you like ketchup and mustard on your hot dog?"

"NO, SIR! I'M FINE!!!" Then she would turn and holler something undecipherable while hurling across our dining room with one roller skate on, wearing pink tights with no shirt.

About three hours of the evening was spent in our daughter's room. If a Toys 'r Us store could vomit, this is what it would look like. I attempted to supervise the delirium, crunching Barbie items along my path to reach the only place safe to sit – the barren toy chest.

One girl sang in a microphone. Three played semi-quietly with the new Barbie Travel Train. About five of them had another girl on the couch, pretending to deliver a baby which they had stuffed under her shirt.

Around 10, the clamor that had threatened to cave in the walls of our home began to diminish to a steady hum. Some laid down to watch a movie, others were still in my daughter's room, piddling in their pajamas.

That my wife was able to lull them all to sleep by 11 was a miracle. She began by reading stories, but that piqued their interest too much and created chatter. Finally, she practiced a lesson from her old husband's book of tricks – "I bored them to sleep," she said.

She simply started counting. "1, 2, 3, 4, 5, then there's 6, then 7, 8, 9, then there's 10..." They were slinging zzzs by 124.

Another miracle occurred during the course of darkness. None of them woke up screaming for their mommy. None of them escaped into the night. We woke at around 7:15 a.m. with everyone and everything intact – even my hair.

The evening, for all its potential for disaster, went surprisingly well. All the girls were sweet and well-mannered. We only had one crying episode (my daughter – the "it's my party and I'll cry if I want to" syndrome). And I didn't have to brandish my gun to restore order once (unlike the last family reunion).

That said, we won't be doing this again anytime soon. Other parents – it's your turn. We've paid my wife's debt to society.

Tantrums, fits and banging your head
May 7, 2003

Legend has it that, as a child, whenever I became frustrated or angry or didn't get my way, I would grab a tree and start banging my head against it.

They tell me that I did this until I was about seven years old. I don't remember banging my head against any trees, or oddly enough, anything prior to the age of eight. But I have no reason to believe, or proof, that they are lying.

This practice apparently caused no long-term damage to my skull or brain. Doctors have concluded that the greenish fluid that regularly seeps from my ears isn't from childhood brain trauma, but rather from a medical condition of unknown origin they refer to as "losing your brains."

I bring up my form of childhood tantrum because my own children are now dabbling in their own fits.

Unlike their father, who selflessly damaged his own cranium rather than bother others with his fury, my children tend to broadcast their emotions for all the tri-county area to enjoy.

This is not something my wife and I particularly like, so we take great pains to stop it. But it's not easy, as most of you parents know.

My four-year-old daughter's newest conniption involves falling on the floor and screaming while churning her arms and legs wildly.

When I first witnessed this move, I thought she was having some type of seizure and quickly rushed to her aid, giving her the Heimlich maneuver (I utilize the Heimlich maneuver on most ailments, including choking, seizures, incessant sneezing, rickets, and tennis elbow. I figure most people forget what ails them when you start pounding their gut).

On the second appearance of this seizure-like fit, I realized it was simply hysterics and adopted the "Andy Griffith" method of dealing with such dander.

On an episode of "The Andy Griffith Show," the new boy, Arnold, showed Opie how a flashy tantrum could elicit all types of goodies from the grown-ups. Opie then went to Andy and asked him for something. When Andy said no, Opie mimicked Arnold's tantrum – stomping his feet, wailing and yelling.

Andy basically ignored him.

Opie realized that the tantrums weren't producing the desired result and quit.

With my daughter, that method works most of the time, but her one-year-old brother hasn't evolved into understanding such manipulation yet.

His outbursts are usually reactions – he doesn't get a cookie he wants, his sister is torturing him, you won't let him jump off a cliff, his sister is torturing him again.

Most of the time, we try to divert his attention or satiate him with something else he likes. You don't want to give him everything he wants, but you don't want to punish him for something he can't understand either.

Soon, though, he will graduate from such innocent huffs, and like all two-year-olds, form his own methods to dupe the old folks into getting what he desires.

We have plenty of big trees in the yard for him, ready for banging.

My one rule, and its exceptions
May 21, 2003

Here is my rule: You are not to call my house between the hours of 11 p.m. and 8 a.m. Conversely, you may call my home between the hours of 8 a.m. and 11 p.m.

As is the case with most rules, there are some exceptions. Under the following scenarios, and ONLY under the following specified scenarios, are you allowed to break my rule, meaning you can call my house at any time if:

1.)   A close relative or friend of mine dies, or you die.

A.) For our purposes, "close relative or friend" will be defined as a person who is related to me or is known to be a close personal friend of mine. That doesn't mean a fourth-cousin I have never met. A barometer to determine if they qualify as a close relative or friend is: Have I ever used the bathroom in their home before? If you believe them to be a relative or a close friend of mine, but doubt I have used their bathroom, their death does not warrant a call between the hours of 11 p.m. and 8 a.m. Err on the side of caution. But if you are absolutely certain that they are a close relative or friend – AND you are absolutely certain I have been in their bathroom, then feel free to call.

In the case of your death, make sure whoever is calling to inform me of the sad news is aware of my rule, and that you are a close relative or friend of mine as defined.

B.) In the case of the death of Hank Aaron or Herschel Walker or Larry Munson, you can call my home at any time to inform me. I have not had the privilege of using their bathrooms, but will need to start mourning immediately, so a prompt call will be appreciated.

2.)   You or a close relative or friend is seriously injured.

For our purposes, we will define "seriously injured" as being admitted, or dragged unconscious, into the intensive care unit of an accredited hospital.

The above definition of "close relative or friend" also applies here. Again, if you are the one seriously injured, please pass along my rule to the person calling on your behalf before they call and wake me up.

3.)   You have earth-shattering news that I must know about.

For our purposes, we will limit "earth-shattering news" to the following: The   earth is actually shattering, and somehow it will affect where I am sleeping; You are a close relative or friend of mine (see definition) and have become engaged to be married (once only); A nuclear bomb is scheduled to hit my county within the next two hours; Georgia football coach Mark Richt has been fired or there is a nasty Internet rumor about him; I have won the lottery and don't know about it yet.

Those are the only cases where the "earth-shattering news" exemption will be accepted.

4.)   Overtime/Extra Innings of a significant sporting event.

You may call my house during the banned hours to tell me the score or merely discuss a significant sporting event that has gone into an overtime/extra inning period. For our purposes, a "significant sporting event" will be limited to the following: A World Series game involving the Atlanta Braves; An NFL playoff game involving the Atlanta Falcons; Any college football game.

5.) You have met Burt Reynolds and he wants to talk to me.

 That is my rule, and those are the exceptions to the rule. I don't have any other rules, so I expect everyone to comply with it.

Non-compliance will result in some type of reaction. For instance, a sister-in-law insisted on breaking my rule, even after I had informed her of it. She would call at 7:15 a.m. and tell me she had to talk to her sister "about something important." She would then tell her sister (my wife) that "You're not going to believe this – I saw a dog yesterday that, if he were human, would look just like Daddy."

I concluded that this bit of information did not meet any of my exemptions. I then acquired her beeper number and proceeded to terrorize her for months – leaving numbers for the bus station, a Chinese massage parlor, Gamblers Anonymous Hotline, her ex-boyfriend, her fourth-grade Math teacher, etc. She would call them, thinking they were somebody who had called her, and tortuous confusion and/or embarrassment would ensue.

I did that for six months or so until she figured out I was behind it. She now obeys my rule.

Being that she was family, I took it easy on her. Now that everyone knows my rule, I expect full compliance – or else.

"You can think about it. But don't do it."
                              -Sheriff Buford T. Justice
                              "Smokey and the Bandit"

Coming Soon: Dr. Lucky's Hot Dog Juice
May 28, 2003

I've always fashioned myself as somewhat of an entrepreneur.

My ventures into entrepreneurship haven't been taken very seriously by society at large, though, probably because, until just recently, I mistakenly believed it was "entremanure" instead of entrepreneur. My mispronunciation, repeated over and over, didn't seem to instill confidence in potential investors.

Now, though, with my corrected enunciation, I have renewed enthusiasm for my latest project.

Unlike my past entrepreneurial projects/inventions – "The Coucherator" (part refrigerator/part couch), "The Ketchupsicle" (the ketchup-flavored popsicle), "The Moth Burger" (Somebody had to find a good use for moths), or "The Fritos-Powered Car" (self-explanatory) – I think I have found the secret to success this time.

First of all, I won't use "The" in the product's name. That seems to be bad luck.

And secondly, my primary downfall in past ventures was that I always got bogged down in complicated scientific minutia (i.e., building a refrigerated couch, freezing ketchup on a stick, catching moths, building a car powered by Fritos, etc.).

This undertaking is so simple even I can make it work. Here's the idea: Hot dog juice.

Whenever I open a package of hot dogs, there is always some juice in the package left over. I have no idea where this juice comes from – probably residue from when they picked them off the tree. I usually just throw the hot dog juice away with the package, or use it to kill weeds in the yard.

My thinking is: People love hot dogs. Nobody is using this juice. Why not sell it?

Hence, Dr. Lucky's 100 Percent Hot Dog Juice.

I don't know who Dr. Lucky is, but I figure putting "Dr. Lucky" in the product's name will lend an aura of credibility to my hot dog juice, as if it's been inspected by an actual medical doctor.

I personally never have consumed any of this hot dog juice, but that's not the point. The point is: If you give a 4-year-old, or an 84-year-old, the choice between prune juice and Dr. Lucky's 100 Percent

Hot Dog Juice, what do you think they are going to choose? Hot dogs trump prunes every time.

I've added the "100 Percent" to the name as part of our marketing strategy to lure health-conscious mothers. When we buy juice at the grocery store, my wife always makes sure it's "100 Percent" juice, and not artificially flavored.

Dr. Lucky's will have no artificial flavors. All of our juice will come straight out of hot dog packages.

With summer now here, who wouldn't want some refreshing hot dog juice with their hot dogs and apple pie. It's a natural.

Why hasn't somebody thought of this before?

Maybe I am Dr. Lucky after all.

My unedited stance on the Pete Rose controversy

August 27, 2003

When readers of this column meet me, they usually ask one of three questions: 1. Are you insane, or just a drunk?; 2. You look much taller in the newspaper (not a question, but I'm not going to split hairs at my height); and 3. How do you write your columns?

Today, as a service to my readers, and because I have nothing else to do, I will answer number 3 and let readers peek in on my column-writing process. Below is a column I wrote for this week in all its unedited glory.

Recently, ~~some guys at the bar~~ sports enthusiasts have revived the controversial debate over whether Pete Rose should be allowed to enter the ~~Bad Hair~~ Baseball Hall of Fame.

Rose, holder of the major league baseball record for most hits in a career, was banned from ~~Hooters~~ baseball (and its Hall of Fame) for ~~an awful haircut~~ allegedly betting on the sport – a big no-no in American's pastime ~~along with taking steroids. He, he~~. Current MLB Commissioner Bud ~~"Bozo" "The Devil"~~ Selig has reportedly been considering allowing Rose to rejoin baseball ~~for a big bundle of cash~~. Whether or not Rose will have to finally admit to betting on baseball games may or may not be a requirement.

There are those ~~morons~~ who believe that because of Rose's stature in the game, he should be allowed to enter the Hall of Fame and return to baseball's good graces. On the other hand, there are others who ~~need a life and~~ are fiercely opposed to his reinstatement, saying he knew the rules and violated them and has been unrepentant about his alleged crimes.

I'm not one to be ~~decisive~~ wishy-washy on any subject at any time ~~except when threatened~~, even if I don't know what the subject is ~~which is always~~. Everyone who follows sports has an opinion on this subject ~~except for me~~. Here is my ~~recipe for chili~~ stand.

First of all, Pete Rose is the greatest singles hitter ~~and baseball gambler~~ of all time. That counts for ~~nothing~~ a little something. From all reports I've seen, he never bet against his own team

~~unless he thought they would lose~~. And while I understand why baseball takes this gambling rule so seriously (the 1919 Black Sox scandal), that was a long time ago ~~(1919, I think)~~. It may be time to change the punishment for that rule ~~(like maybe a caning, a flogging, or a good haircut)~~. A permanent banishment may be too ~~meek~~ harsh in this particular case.

So, with the above in mind, I definitely ~~don't~~ think that Rose should be reinstated to baseball and be immediately eligible for the ~~Bad Hair~~ Hall of Fame.

But, as stated, Rose knew the rules (they are posted everywhere) and purposely and deliberately violated them ~~if indeed he can read, which is questionable~~. He has shown no remorse, no contrition ~~no sense to get a new hairstyle~~. If we allow Rose back into baseball without him even admitting the error of his ways (which is ~~his hair~~ obvious, despite his contentions), then how long will it be before another World Series is fixed ~~or baseball players start taking steroids. He, he.~~ ?

So, I certainly ~~disagree agree don't care disagree~~ agree with those who believe Pete Rose should remain banned for the game.

That is my ~~long, incoherent diatribe~~ stance. I will ~~probably~~ not retreat from it.

Art through the eyes of a four-year-old
September 3, 2003

"Every child is an artist..."

In the same week, my four-year-old daughter started Pre-Kindergarten and we found out my wife was pregnant. The congruence of these two events has prompted a drastic increase in blubbering and sniffling during deodorant commercials and wailings of "my little girl is growing up too fast!"

And my wife has been fairly emotional too.

Our daughter has quickly adapted to her first public schooling experience, and is now bringing home some of her school work each Friday. Her school work of the first three weeks has mostly consisted of her drawings, or as they say in England, "drawer-reens."

At the bottom of each of these drawings, her teacher has put down a brief explanation of what our daughter contends the drawing is.

Here is what she brought home this week:

• Some zig-zagging black lines horizontally up and down a page, with some more lines in a scribbling pattern positioned vertically in the upper right-hand corner. According to our daughter, this is a picture of "Flowers talking to one another."

• A circle with lines drawn inside it, going basically everywhere. This is "A monster. The cowboy is trying to lock him up."

• A green circle in the upper left-hand corner. In the upper right-hand corner are a bunch of scribbly pink and blue lines.
This is "A baby turtle on its mother's back."

• Pink and blue lines up and down a page vertically are a "pink and blue swimming pool."

• A bunch of purple and green lines going in every possible direction are "a Barbie."

• One line going diagonally across the page, with different lines intersecting it every two inches are also "a swimming pool."

• Two lines running parallel – one blue, one red with a little purple in it: "A Barbie beach."

• Two squares side-by-side. "A Barbie window," of course.

Some of the drawings did not have captions underneath them. I beckoned my daughter to my chair to entitle her creations.

"What's this?" I asked of what looked like two footballs without any laces.

"That's a rabbit and a mouse."

The next picture was of a couple of purple circles at the top, and then one large pink circle toward the bottom of the page, with a bunch of scribbling inside.

I asked "What is this?"

She turned the tables on me. "What do you think it is, Daddy?"

"Well, it looks sort of like an international-rules basketball court. See, there's that weird-looking free-throw line."

"No, that's not a Frito line," she said in the same 'you're wrong, again' voice used frequently by her mother. "It's a Barbie swimming pool. You don't see what I see."

Unfortunately, she was right.

"...the problem is how to remain an artist once he grows up."
                                                                    - Pablo Picasso

The case of the missing remote control

The crime: Theft of my remote control.

The remote control has been missing for 13 days. It was last seen on the arm of my chair in my living room. I had just refreshed the duct tape over the back of the remote control (which holds the battery lid on), and placed it gently on the chair's arm. I left the room, and haven't seen my remote control since.

The suspects:

• My wife, age somewhere between 24 and 31.

More than once, has said that she has no need for television. A background check showed no Communist Party affiliations. Despite her heretical proclamations, she's compulsive about watching HGTV – which I call "The Effeminate Channel." That's the only channel she watches, which raises suspicions about whether she destroyed the remote control so she could watch just that network.

Claims she loves me and would never do such a thing, but is prone to get mad about little things, like when I wiped the fudgesicle drippings from my chin on that quilt her great-grandmother made. Makes me question that "love you" thing she keeps saying.

• Daughter, age 4.

Can't get a straight answer out of her, which is troubling. Was very evasive when questioned. My attempts at torturing it out of her were futile. Interrogation while holding her by her ankles over the toilet produced nothing but repeated pleas of "Daddy, hold me upside down over the potty again?"

Doesn't know how to properly operate remote control, but respects its power. Have seen her get frustrated when Daddy won't get off the couch to turn it to *Nickelodeon*, which means she would probably produce the remote if she knew where it is.

• Son, age 1.

He's almost two, which is when children learn to lie, cheat and steal. Doesn't speak English well. May need to get 2 1/2-year-old translator for questioning. Has shown a propensity to hide things. Found my wedding band in his diaper once. Searched his regular hiding places (toy box, under couch, in his mother's jewelry box, in the laundry basket, in his mouth) to no avail.

Hard to break. He loves torture. Currently, the chief suspect.

• Old man down the street.

Sunday afternoon, he asked me if "I watched the game?" He never asked me that before, so it's possible he did that to get a rise out of me - knowing he stole my remote control.

As incriminating as that is, he uses a walker, and I don't think he could climb the steps to get in our house without help. An accomplice could be involved.

• Anonymous letter writer who hates me.

Every once in a while, I get a letter from this person who detests me and goes on and on about how awful my columns are. At first, I suspected a relative, but this person obviously doesn't know me. If they did, they would know that I consider being called "sophomoric" a compliment.

No sign of a ransom note - yet.

The investigation is ongoing, so I can't really comment on the details of the probe. If you see my remote control (it's black with small buttons on it), or know of someone who has, please contact your local law enforcement authorities at once.

They are aware of this crime, and said they would get around to investigating it right after they finish with all the unsolved murders.

Aiming for my own world record
February 4, 2004

It's about time I did something with my life.

Like Dean Gould of England, who has set world records for coin snatching (328), beer mat throwing (2,204), beer mat flipping (111 with one hand, 65 with both hands), pancake tossing (399 in three minutes), stamp licking (309 in five minutes), needle threading (3,471 times within two hours), eating 63 grapes with a plastic teaspoon in three minutes, eating 51 grains of rice with chopsticks in three minutes, eating 113 pieces of sweet corn with a cocktail stick in three minutes, eating three dry cream crackers (3:07), and picking 50 winkles from their shells (1:22).

That would be even more impressive if I knew what a beer mat, a dry cream cracker, or a winkle was.

Call it a midlife crisis, or boredom, but I feel a need to have my name etched in the world record book, along the likes of Rev. Dr. Donald Thomas, who holds two world records: Longest sermon (93 hours – called "God's Filibuster"), and longest after-dinner speech (32 hours – called "Remind Me to Never Invite This Guy to Dinner Again").

I've had half-hearted attempts before. A couple of years ago, I tried to convince the Guinness Book of World Records that I owned the largest holly bush on earth. The nitwits never responded to my claim, focusing instead of drivel like the world's biggest foot (Matthew McGrory, size 28 1/2 shoe).

So, I have searched through standing world records and have a few I am considering attempting to break. Listed for your perusal are my considerations, with their perceived pros and cons.

• Standing motionless. India's Akshinthala Seshu Babu currently holds the record, standing motionless for 30 hours, 12 minutes.

Pro: Last time my wife told me she was pregnant, I stood perfectly motionless for nearly an hour without even trying.

Con: Would interfere with eating.

• Non-stop recital of the Complete Works of Shakespeare.

Adrian Hilton set the world record by reciting Shakespeare for over 110 hours.

Pro: Don't think I could memorize complete works of Shakespeare, but I could do a complete recital of Jackie Gleason's lines in "Smokey and the Bandit," "Smokey and the Bandit II," and "Smokey and the Bandit III."

Con: I'm sure somebody's already done that.

• Beer Keg Lifting.

Austria's Friedrich Konrad set the record, picking up a 349-pound keg of beer.

Pro: Lots of experience from college.

Con: That was a long time ago. And in college, I lifted the keg after I drank it. I think this keg would be full.

• Non-stop push-ups.

Japan's Minora Yoshida holds the current world record, doing 10,507 push-ups.

Pro: Would be a great way to get in shape.

Con: To gauge the plausibility of challenging this record, I tested myself on how many push-ups I could do the other day. I did four.

• Joggling relay.

Joggling is a combination of jogging and juggling – no kidding. Meike Duch and Andreas Lietzow of Germany set the world record by joggling with three balls for 109 miles.

Pro: These dudes obviously made "joggling" up. I could combine two things I do well and set a world record.

Con: Don't know if the world-record folks will take "layting" (laying down while eating) too seriously.

But I'll give it a world-record try. Wish me luck.

I'd like my kidney back now
March 3, 2004

An amazing, true story: A guy my wife went to high school with needed a kidney.

A young, athletic guy (former Georgia football player), was on a transplant waiting list, with not a lot of time to spare. His brother had gone through the process to donate a kidney, but didn't match. His wife decided to give it a try. Against long, long odds, she was a perfect match.

So, last week, the wife donated her kidney to her husband. The transplant was a success, and both husband and wife are reportedly doing very well.

Prayers were answered, for sure. And it looks like we have a blissful, happy ending.

But the husband in me senses a potential problem.

For example, my wife recently gave birth to our third child. The other day, I'm lying around when my wife calls me to fix a doorknob.

Why she called me, I don't know. Apparently, the door wouldn't open anymore and one of the kids was locked outside in the cold in his underwear. Problem was, I was embroiled in VH-1's "I Love the '70s: 1978" – possibly the greatest year ever for pop culture. They were about to talk about "Animal House." Not the proper time to abandon the television.

When beckoned again, I replied, "Uh, you're going to have to wait a little bit. I'm busy right now."

This prompted the following retort, which I've heard in one form or another once a day for the last five years: "Well, I wasn't too busy to give birth to your child two weeks ago." Another variation of that is when she points out how long she was in labor, as in: "I think you can sit through 'Steel Magnolias' for another hour since I was in labor with your child for 16 hours!" The length of her labor is squared each year of the child's life – starts out at four hours; the next year it's 16, and so on. Meaning that when the child is 25, my wife will claim she was in labor the entirety of that child's life. Although at that point, this ploy will be used on the child, not me – "I was in labor with you for 25 years and you don't even call me on Bastille Day?"

How can you answer that? How can a husband justify the physical ordeal of folding towels vs. the physical ordeal of childbirth?

"I – I take out the garbage" just doesn't cut it. Neither does "I washed the dishes once last week." Trust me – I've tried it.

Unless I go through some physical turmoil on her behalf – which I don't see happening – I'm always going to come out on the short end of the pain and suffering stick.

Which leads me to the friend whose wife gave him a kidney. How is he ever going to answer that?

I mean, after a while – probably 40-or-so years, or when the child gets a nose ring – the "I gave birth to your children" gambit loses its punch. Not so with a kidney.

Don't want to take out the garbage? "Well, I think I'll just take back my kidney."

Don't want to go with me to see Clay Aiken in concert? "Well, that isn't what my kidney said. It said 'I'm ready to go.'"

You don't like the taste of those mashed potatoes? "Well, your body sure likes my kidney."

Basically, any argument can be ended, and lost by the husband, with: "Didn't I give you my kidney?"

In the hands of a wily woman, such ammunition could be brutal.

Luckily, in this case, the wife isn't the least bit devious (heck, she gave him her kidney). But if she decided to be cunning, there would be nothing he could do.

What if I gave my wife my gall bladder? Perhaps as an anniversary present? Would that make us even?

No, it certainly wouldn't. I've seen what it takes to give birth.

That said, I have no interest in being even.

Sleepwalking: The way to get things done

I have sleepwalked twice in my life.

The first time, I was nine. I got out of bed, walked downstairs, passed my parents watching television in the den, and went into the laundry room. As I reached into the dryer, my parents asked me what I was doing.

"I'm getting something to drink," I responded vehemently. I then walked upstairs and went back to sleep.

My second sleepwalking episode happened about two months ago. My wife tells me that she woke up in the middle of the night to find me standing at the foot of the bed, muttering and gesturing.

"What are you doing?"

I then turned to her and said plainly, "You don't have to worry about me ever playing cards with you again." I then rolled back into bed, or so she says.

The next day, when she told me of my nocturnal declaration, I didn't remember it at all – or a dream where I vowed to never play cards with someone.

Although I've never been much of a sleepwalker, I've known a few. A friend of mine used to sleepwalk nightly, and actually do things while he was sleepwalking. I would be at his apartment, hanging out with his roommate, and sleepwalking Daniel would come out of his bedroom and sometimes actually clean up or do chores. If you spoke to him, he would scream at you, usually something nonsensical like: "I've never been to Finland, dummy!"

And then he would wander off into the bathroom to scrub the toilet.

This sleepwalking talk got me to thinking, which I rarely do while awake. Why can't I get myself to sleepwalk and do all the things I don't like to do while fully conscious? It would be the ultimate in multi-tasking. If I could accomplish at least 90 percent of my daily tasks while sleepwalking, I could get done almost half of what a normal person does while they are awake.

For instance, Sleepwalking Me would do all the things I don't like to do: Take out the trash, replace blown lightbulbs, change diapers, wash clothes, balance the checkbook, drive the kids to school, go to work, talk to people, etc.

Awake Me would then be able to concentrate on the things I need to do, but don't currently have enough time to do because I sleep 10 hours a night. Things like: Read a book (all of it), waterski, watch more of "The Simpsons," finish that sequel to "Big Trouble in Little China" I've been writing, spend more time with the kids, figure out how to stop that timer on the VCR from flashing 12:01 all the time, and finally learn to breakdance.

Problem is, it's hard to find someone to hypnotize you into becoming a sleepwalking multi-tasker. I've tried. Right after I concocted this brilliant scheme, I went to a hypnotist, got hypnotized, but nothing has changed – other than I start quacking like a duck and jump into water whenever someone says "tornado" (or so the police officer said).

I can't let the dream of the industrious Sleepwalking Me die, though. If you know a hypnotist that doesn't revel in cruel practical jokes, let me know. I'm putting off mowing the grass in hopes that I'll realize my dream soon. Awake Me just isn't up to it.

The angst of entering 'big school' revisited
August 11, 2004

"Daddy, I don't want to go to the big school."

This was uttered about a month ago as we verbally prepared our five-year-old daughter for her entrance into kindergarten, which is housed at the elementary school – "big school" to the Pre-K set.

"Why not? I thought you liked school," I replied softly.

"I'm scared of the big kids," my daughter – who may be 35 pounds with lots of heavy clothes on – intimated. "I'm too little to go to big school."

I wrapped my arm around her skinny shoulders and the wax turned nostalgic.

"Let me tell you a story. It's the story of my first day of school," I started. "Back then, we didn't have kindergarten in the big school. First grade was when you went to the big school."

"Where did you go to kindergarten then?" she interrupted.

"I went to kindergarten in Mrs. Frisbee's basement," I replied rather bitterly. "She once locked me in her closet for jumping on her couch. Apparently, there were no laws preventing such mistreatment back then. So I retaliated by taking her vacuum cleaner apart. But that's another story.

"Anyway, back to my first day of school. Unlike all those other little pansies who had their parents take them to school the first day, I rode the bus to school the first day. You've ridden a school bus before, haven't you?"

My daughter nodded in the affirmative. "Lots of times, in Pre-K," she said.

"Right. And you could get on the bus all by yourself, right?"

"Yes, all by myself," she said.

"Right. Well, you know what? On my first day of school, and I was a year older than you are now, you know what happened when I tried to get on that school bus the first day?"

"It ran over you?"

"No, it didn't run over me," I replied. "I was so small, so tiny, that I couldn't get up that first step by myself."

"Really? You were that little?"

"Yes, I was. Smaller than you are now," I told her. "The bus driver, this nice lady, got out of her seat, picked me up like a little baby, and put me in the seat right behind her."

She was looking at me liked I had invented popsicles.

"She picked you up like a baby? You were as little as a baby? Did she pick you up because you couldn't walk yet?"

"No, I wasn't as small as a baby, and I could walk, but I was smaller than you. And I did just fine at the big school. There were other kids even smaller than me," I told her.

That seemed to ease her apprehension a bit.

Weeks later, we accompanied her to the "big school" for the first day of kindergarten. Some tears were shed – predominantly by her mother – but they were quickly wiped away by the joy of a new classroom to explore. Within minutes, all angst about being the smallest kid in a big school was lost.

Yesterday, I asked my daughter about her second day of school and how it went. She told me she loved it and recounted a few of the school day's events. A few minutes passed, then she added: "You know what, Daddy. There were some kids that were smaller than me, just like you said."

"I told you," I replied. "And soon enough, you'll grow up to be as big as the big kids, just like I did."

She mulled this over for a moment, pointed at my gut, then said: "Daddy, I don't want to grow as big as you."

Where was Mrs. Frisbee's closet when I needed it?

Dropped to third on the smart depth chart
September 8, 2004

I consider myself a fairly smart guy.

I almost failed only one grade in elementary school, made a C in Italian in college, and once finished the *People* magazine crossword puzzle in 15 minutes flat.

Don't get me wrong. I'm no Norman Einstein. But I can read about anything that doesn't take too long and am able to get out of jury duty most of the time.

But even with my slightly-better-than-stupid intellect, I will be the first to admit that women outsmart me daily. Starting at home.

For instance, like every married couple, once in a while, my wife and I will disagree on a topic. It can be something as simple as me saying: "This month is September." My wife will dispute my statement, insisting that it's still August. I'll then back up my claim with evidence, providing a calendar, computer printouts, a phone call to the time guy, and affidavits signed by Morris Day and the Time, all testifying that the current month is most definitely September.

Yet, for some reason, when all is said and done, I end up agreeing with her and apologizing for insisting otherwise, and also apologizing for something I did three years ago.

The thing is: I can handle living in a house with one woman that can outsmart me. I'm used to it. The problem is: I think there are now two of them in our home.

The other day, my five-year-old daughter and two-year-old son took all the pillows off of every couch, chair and bed in our house – making what they call "Pillow World" in our living room. After their last foray into "Pillow World," which occurred two hours earlier, they were expressly forbidden from building another "Pillow World."

When engaged about the renewed presence of "Pillow World," my daughter replied that her brother did it all on his own accord, and her brother said his sister "made me help her." Both were given the same punishment: No TV that night. And they had to deconstruct "Pillow World," which was almost as fun as making it.

After "Pillow World" was destroyed, my daughter eased up to my wife and said, "Mommy, I have to tell you something."

"Okay," my wife said. "What?"

"It was my idea to build Pillow World again," my daughter admitted.

"Well, I'm glad you told me the truth," my wife said. "You should always tell the truth. But you also lied to me, telling us your brother built it by himself. So, the punishment still stands. No TV."

My daughter sighed, then walked off.

About 10 minutes later, she returned.

"Mommy, I need to tell you something."

"Okay," my wife said. "What?"

"Well, I've been thinking about lying about Pillow World," my daughter said. "And there's a TV show on tonight about lying. I think I need to watch it so I can see how bad it is. Is that okay?"

Now, whether my daughter was talking about the Republican National Convention, I don't know.

Either way, my wife didn't fall for it. She stuck to the punishment.

On the other hand, if I were to have been approached with the same scenario, I would have bought it hook, line, sinker and pole.

"You want to watch a show about lying? Sure, that sounds like a great idea! Television can teach us so much. Can I watch too? Let's make some popcorn."

Like I said, I'm a dummy.

And I don't think I'm going to be much help to my wife when our daughter is 14.

Capisce?

Things to do during a hurricane
September 15, 2004

Two weeks ago, an ex-hurricane named Frances sauntered through our hamlet, dumping water, trees and trouble along its path.

With power out for hours and our family stuck, literally, in the mud, I learned three valuable lessons previously unknown. They are: 1. The television doesn't work without power (a crushing blow); 2. To children, Monopoly game pieces are good eatin'; and 3. Hardly any televisions are battery-operated.

I will not be unprepared again. With another possible hurricane/tropical storm on our doorstep, I am currently in the midst of preparations to alleviate the hellish boredom that comes with being without power, without light, without a microwave oven, without TV, VCR, or AC, but with a bunch of people stuck in a hot room with nothing to do.

My wife finds the lack of modern amenities endearing – a chance to interact and be creative without the squawk of contemporary convenience.

She envisions inviting family members over to our house to sit around in the dark and talk, engage in light-hearted banter, play games, or participate in popular sing-a-longs like "Kumbayah," "Michael Row the Boat Ashore" or "Yammo Be There" – which was, according to news reports, one of Saddam Hussein's favorite methods of torture.

I'd rather stick a giant T-square up my rear (another Saddam fave).

Don't get me wrong. I love my family; love being around them. But I can't be around anybody for more than five hours at a single sitting, even myself. That's why I take a nap every four hours.

Thus, I have prepared a listing of some things you can do during a hurricane to break up the monotony, have some fun, and preserve your sanity.

You are welcome in advance.

• Darts.

Darts don't require any electricity. All you need is a dart and a board, and if you have children, a suit of rigid armor.

While fun during the daytime, the merriment multiplies with no lighting.

• Hide-and-Seek.

Kids love Hide-and-Seek, and adults can too, if they know how to play.

Here's what I do: Right before you're about to play, grab a good book and a flashlight. When you hide, lock yourself in the bathroom or a closet or in the attic. Those boneheads won't find you for hours.

• Cards.

If you're stuck in the house for hours, you might as well make a buck.

Break the piggy-banks, put the candles on the dining room table, and start a lengthy round of Texas Hold 'Em (Sidenote: Most kids under six don't know the rules of Texas Hold 'Em, which could be an advantage if you can find some to play).

• Contests that provoke sleep.

I love sleeping during storms. Problem is, I always have all these people running around my house, yelling and stuff. The goal is: Get everybody else to sleep too. For children, you have to wear them out. One way to do that is contests. Some surefire suggestions include: Push-up or pull-up contests (children are notoriously weak); Night boxing (a knockout is a form of sleep); Spinning contests (first kid to pass out wins!); Drinking games (warm milk laced with Benadryl).

For adults, I'd suggest the following, in order: drinking games (substituting Benadryl with vodka), then spinning contests, more drinking games, then night boxing.

Remember: If you fail to prepare, you prepare to fail. Or is it the other way around?

Parents be stupider after birthins
September 22, 2004

You've seen it before, or done it before, or done seen it before.

You've seen the parent at the little league baseball game who's got their nose sticking through the chain-link fence, yelling at the coach for not playing their son. Or the parent who gets belligerent with the teacher when their child is punished for misbehavior.

"My son is the best player on the team! Why isn't he playing!"

"My daughter would never do that. You're wrong!"

Probably sounds familiar, especially to those who coach or teach.

I used to chalk that type of parent behavior to one of two reasons:

1. The parent loves their child so much they are blind to the truth; or
2. The parent is a jerk.

Now I know better. The parents are simply big dummies.

This from Indiana University: A five-year study concludes that having children significantly lowers a parent's IQ.

Well, no duh!

Researchers started the study in 1999 with 200 couples who planned on starting families, giving each prospective parent an IQ test (IQ stands for Important Questions – I think. I used to know before I became a parent). By 2003, all but 27 of those couples had children. Then, their IQs were measured again. In all 173 cases, both parents scored at least 12 points lower on the second IQ test. And most of the parents had become even stupider than that.

This is what the director of the study, Dr. Hosung Lee, said of the findings, according to published reports: "The research proved that our hypothesis was correct. Having children does retard one's brain activity, and since both parents lost intelligence, we must assume that this loss has a psychological rather than biological cause."

According to the study, the part of the brain that makes one think objectively loses the most brainpower once a child enters the scene.

"This explains why every parent thinks their child is the smartest kid in class or the best athlete, even if that child is as dumb as a box of rocks or needs a calendar to time their 40-yard dash," Dr. Lee is quoted as saying, obviously full of himself for proving something that was blatantly obvious, even to a dumb parent like me.

This news, as expected as it was, is indeed scary. What about those of us who can't afford to lose much brainpower? I've got three kids – that means I've lost at least... twenty-nine, no, forty-five, uh... well, a lot of brainy points, or whatever they be called. What's going to happen when Pauly Shore has children? Or Britney Spears? Egads, she got married last week. That's what the Enquirer said. It's got to be true.

Cartoons make me laugh.

Look, when I press these buttons on the thingy-ma-jing, little letters pop up on the television set in front of me. Wow.

My shirt tastes yummy.

I don't believe this man with the funny name who says parents be dumb and stuff. You do too?

Who wouldn't love a singing bass?

December 1, 2004

In a moment of weakness, she struck.

Giddy from our local high school football team's win in the Dome Friday, my wife slipped in the following: "I'm so happy we won. Now, we can finish off a great trip by Christmas shopping on the way home. It will be fun! Okay?"

"Okay," I replied, football drunk and not in my right mind.

So, on Saturday, instead of spending my day doing something worthwhile and meaningful, like sleeping or watching football, or both, I slogged from place to place down I-75 on a shopping expedition.

Let's get this straight from the get-go: I enjoy shopping about as much as I enjoy sticking my big toe in a garbage disposal, which I do rarely. On the other hand, my wife absolutely loves shopping. She can spend an entire weekend shopping and not buy a thing. What a grand concept. Think I'll try it next weekend. I'll tell her I'm doing "yard work" all weekend and not accomplish anything.

Heck, that does sound like fun.

Anyway, I've found there are only two things I can do on a shopping trip with my wife: 1. Participate in an effort to get it over quicker; or B. Sit in the car, read the paper, and wait.

The problems with number 1. are many and messy.

First, we have three children, ages five, two and nine months. While my wife scours every nook and cranny for the perfect gift, I am often stuck in the role of babysitter. Two observations: One, there are a lot of great places to hide in a department store. And my children found them all. Secondly, shoplifting isn't as difficult as it would seem – if you're two.

In an effort to expedite my wife's laborious shopping pace, I asked for a list of people to buy things for. I was presented a list of five people to buy Christmas presents for at 1:10 p.m. At 1:19 p.m., I returned to my wife with a cart full of yuletide presents.

One by one, my wife nixed my gift ideas, leaving my cart empty and my mind befuddled. I ask you: Who wouldn't love a singing bass?

After giving up on babysitting and helping with the shopping, I found myself wandering around aimlessly. This is also dangerous. Lost in a daze, I found myself in the women's lingerie section. It always sneaks up on you. A 72-year-old woman gave me the evil eye. Or maybe she was winking at me. I didn't stick around to find out.

So I tried B. – sitting in the car and waiting.

After I read the paper twice, the kids – who were also banished with me – started to get fidgety. After cutting every piece of paper in the car into little, teeny pieces, a plastic sword fight commenced, then a war of words.

My five-year-old daughter called her two-year-old brother a "geek" – her favored putdown this week. Her brother continuously countered with his new expression – "your butt smells." The baby screamed for the comforting rattle of the road, where he prefers to sleep.

Finally, I had enough. I strapped them into their seats and issued my edict.

"You are not to speak to one another again. If you want to talk to me, fine. Or talk to yourself, fine. But neither of you is to speak to the other, and that means calling each other names."

The car radio was the only noise heard for probably two minutes.

Then my two-year-old son interrupted the peace.

"Daddy," he whispered.

"Yes, son," I said, turning around. I looked deep into his eyes. Right above his right pupil, I could see a monkey speed up on a treadmill.

"Daddy, will you tell her that her butt smells?"

Knowing the essential current events
January 5, 2005

Recently, I read an investigative report detailing how little young people knew about current events, politics and government.

The disturbing story, which I believe was in last month's *Tiger Beat,* stated that more than 50 percent of teens didn't even know the President of the United States was, you know, that guy on TV.

As a newspaperman, current events are my business. If our young people aren't concerned or interested in current events and what's going on in their world and community, I'm toast.

So I cornered two young people to test their knowledge of current events – to see if *Tiger Beat* got it right, or if they were once again engaging in muckraking tabloid journalism.

Below is the transcript of my interview:

Me: Okay, for the record, please state your ages as of today.

My daughter: Five.

My son: (Holding up two fingers and his thumb) Three!

Me: Good. You each got at least one answer correct. That's a good start. Okay, now on to the tough stuff. What country do you live in?

Daughter: Georgia.

Son: Firefighter!

Me: Wrong. But you were close, honey. The answer is United States of America. Okay, now, who is the President of the United States of America?

Daughter: George Washington.

Son: Batman!

Me: Wrong, although George Washington was close. His name is George W. Bush. Okay, now the vice president. Who is the vice president?

Daughter: What's a vice precedent?

Me: It's like the assistant president.

Daughter: What does a precedent do?

Me: He's the boss of the country.

Daughter: No he isn't. God is the boss of the country.

Me: Okay, yeah, I guess you're right. But who is the vice president?

Daughter: Abraham Lincoln.

Son: Spiderman!

Me: No, it's not Abraham Lincoln or Spiderman. It's Dick Cheney.

Daughter: So, Mr. George is the vice precedent's boss?

Son: No, Spiderman!

Me: Yes, and that's exactly how Mr. George pronounces vice president. Okay, what state do you live in?

Daughter: Homerville.

Son: Firefighter!

Me: No, Homerville is the city you live in. And Homerville is in the state of Georgia.

Daughter: Are we done yet? Where's the cookies you promised?

Me: Hold on. Just a few more questions. Okay, what year is it? Now remember, the year just changed.

Daughter: 1999.

Son: Three!

Me: No, it just changed to 2005.

Daughter: Why?

Me: Because at the end of December, it becomes January and a new year.

Daughter: Why?

Me: I don't know. That's just the way it is. Let's move on. Okay, what country were we recently at war with?

Daughter: The United Steaks of America.

Son: Superman!

Me: It's United States of America, honey. And we live in the United States of America.

Daughter: Why are we at war with where we live?

Me: No, we were at war with Iraq.

Daughter: A rock? Why were we at war with a rock?

Me: No, I-rack. It's a country a long way away.

Son: My butt just burped!

Me: Okay, okay. Let's move on to something else.

Daughter: So, does the precedent decide what year it is, or God?

Me: Who played recently for the college football national championship?

Daughter: What division?

Me: Division 1-A.

Daughter: USC and Oklahoma.

Son: No! Trojans and Sooners!

Me: Yes and yes. You're both right. And you both passed your current events quiz with flying colors.

Hugs and cookies followed.

The future of America, and newspapering, is indeed bright – as long as we keep having a sports page.

Making sense, or nonsense, out of 'Levon'
April 20, 2005

These songs we sing along to – what do they mean?

What exactly are we humming? And what point are the songwriters trying to make?

Usually, I have no idea. Heck, I thought Neil Diamond was singing about some guy named "Reverend Eugene," – not "Forever in Blue Jeans."

Curious – okay, bored – I decided to dig up the lyrics to a song which I have never understood and whose meaning always baffled me – Elton John's "Levon."

Below, in italics, are the lyrics to "Levon," written by John and Bernie Taupin, for us to examine:

Levon wears his war wound like a crown

He calls his child Jesus

'Cause he likes the name

And he sends him to the finest school in town

Okay, so this Levon fellow was in a war. He names his son Jesus, and he sends him to a private school. That makes sense, although I wouldn't name a child Jesus. That's asking for trouble. Every time someone stubs their toe and yells "Jesus!," this kid is going to be jumping out of his drawers. And he's liable to get the big head, thinking all those hymns are about him.

Levon, Levon likes his money

He makes a lot they say

Spends his days counting

In a garage by the motorway

Okay, so Levon is rich, and doesn't have an accountant. Got it.

He was born a pauper to a pawn on a Christmas Day

When the New York Times said God is dead

And the wars begun

Alvin Tostig has a son today

This is where the confusion sets in.

So, Levon is born on Christmas Day. And then the *New York Times,* on Christmas Day, said God is dead, which started wars? Actually, German philosopher Friedrich Nietzsche said "God is dead," – back in something like 1890 (I had to look it up). And it didn't start any wars.

And who is Alvin Tostig? Levon's father, I'm left to assume. So

Jesus' name is Jesus Tostig? Urgh.

And he shall be Levon
And he shall be a good man
And he shall be Levon
In tradition with the family plan
And he shall be Levon
And he shall be a good man
He shall be Levon

Enough already. We'll call him Levon.

Levon sells cartoon balloons in town
His family business thrives
Jesus blows up balloons all day
Sits on the porch swing watching them fly

Wait, I thought Levon was supposed to be rich? Selling cartoon balloons? I can understand being wealthy if you were a cartoon balloon manufacturer, but this Levon guy just sells them. Is there really that big a market for balloons shaped like Daffy Duck? And his kid blows the balloons up and lets them fly off. How is Levon making a profit?

And Jesus, he wants to go to Venus
Leaving Levon far behind
Take a balloon and go sailing
While Levon, Levon slowly dies

So, apparently, Jesus doesn't like Levon too much, seeing as how he wants to leave him behind to slowly die.

But why does he want to fly a balloon to, of all places, Venus? From what I hear, it's very cold there. I guess the songwriting decision came down to: What rhymes with Jesus? Panama City – nope. Vegas, nah. How 'bout Venus? There you go.

While the song doesn't indicate if Levon is cruel or mean, it does give us one clue as to why Levon wouldn't be held in such high regard by his son – he named him Jesus Tostig! If he would have named him Ted or Earl or Skip, the kid would probably love his father and wouldn't let all those balloons go flying off.

The point of the song? What does "Levon" tell us? Hmm, I've narrowed it down to two possible themes:

1. Don't name you son Jesus Tostig.
He'll hate you.

2. Elton John and Bernie Taupin were on dope.

You make you own determination. I'm leaning heavily toward 2.

New species could just be monkey business
May 25, 2005

Scientists had basically given up on the pursuit for new species of animal on this earth of ours. The last new finding had occurred way back in 1975 with the startling discovery of Danny DeVito.

That is, until recently.

Suddenly, new phylums are popping up like letters from Nigerians in my e-mail box.

Last week, it was reported that scientists from the University of Georgia and other institutions discovered a new species of monkey in the African country of Tanzania. Giddy scientists – who never get to name anything anymore – dubbed the new species the highland mangabey. Drunk scientists decided its scientific name would be Lophocebus Kipunji – which, ironically, was my nickname in high school.

No scientists could be reached for comment last week on the monkey because all of them were camping out in line to watch the premiere of "Revenge of the Sith," but reports describe the monkey as "brown with some white on its belly."

This news comes on the heels of two more sensational discoveries in the animal kingdom: The revelation of a previously-unknown species of rodent in Southeast Asia; and the surprising reemergence of the ivory-billed woodpecker in Arkansas – previously thought extinct.

The ivory-billed woodpecker is "a woodpecker on steroids," according to one ornithologist (which, even more surprising, is not an eye doctor). The ivory-billed woodpecker is the largest woodpecker in North America, and third-largest in the world. Believed to have been extinct since the 1940s, it suddenly re-emerged in eastern Arkansas recently, obviously lured back into civilization by the sudden availability of steroids not being utilized by Barry Bonds.

As a cynical pseudo-journalist, my response to all this "new animal" hoopla is cynicism. I simply don't buy it.

First of all, from the reports I read, none of these scientists actually caught any of these animals, nor did they shoot them and then study their dead carcasses in a lab. If they just saw a bunch of monkeys from afar, how do they definitively know that they are a new breed of monkey? They said they were "brown with some white." How do they know they weren't just dirty monkeys, or Muppets playing a prank? They've been known to do that.

As for the ivory-billed woodpecker, I have some more probing questions. For instance, if this is the biggest woodpecker in all of North America, I find it unfathomable that nobody has seen it for 60 years. I don't know if you are aware of this, but woodpeckers are called woodpeckers because they peck on wood. They make a lot of racket. Arkansas has some desolate regions, but somebody should have heard something over the last six decades.

I've been to Arkansas, have family there, visit the state often. You can drive from one side to the other in less than five hours. I find it hard to believe that the federal government spent seven years and $70 million investigating that Whitewater thing in Arkansas back in the '90s and not one of those investigators saw the biggest, loudest woodpecker on the continent.

Then again, they couldn't find anything on Bill or Hillary Clinton either, so that's quite understandable.

As a cynical pseudo-journalist, I live by the creed: "If it's too good to be true, it probably is."

Now, you will have to please excuse me. I have some business to attend to with the Honorable Clement Okon of Nigeria, who has promised me the princely sum of $1.5 million (U.S.) for simply helping him out of a legal quandary.

The anatomy of a perfect nap
July 13, 2005

There are some folks who don't like to nap.

I categorize them with the other "People I Don't Understand": The French; job-seekers with visible tattoos; vegetarians; the Los Angeles Clippers; Garth Brooks fans; and the 4,306 people that voted for Michael Dukakis in 1988.

Obviously, people who don't appreciate a good nap simply aren't working hard enough.

I mean, after five days a week, six hours a day, of laboring in front of the computer, my body is exhausted, my brain frazzled from all that reading, napping, and talking on the phone. Ten hours of sleep a night just doesn't suffice. I need at least two naps over the weekend to truly be fit and rested.

Well, okay, just rested.

I've been napping since the day I was born, and, man, there have been some great ones along the way. Like Hank Aaron when discussing what's the most memorable of his 755 home runs, I can't really pinpoint one nap that sticks out as the very best or the most enjoyable. All are enjoyable in their own wonderful way.

The secret to a soothing siesta – like most everything – is in its preparation. While all nappers have their own preferences, styles, and tastes, the elements of proper respite have to be in place for the most splendid of slumbers. Let me explain the essences of my most satisfying snoozes.

First of all, there is a difference between the vacation nap and the home nap.

The best kind of nap is the beach nap. You spend an active morning on the beach in the sun with your family, or perhaps some strangers. After a hearty noon meal, you retire to solitary sleeping quarters. For the best naps, I would suggest making sure your reservation calls for a beachview on an upper floor with a sliding glass door. That way, prior to napping, you can open the sliding glass door, partially close the curtains, and have an ocean breeze for which to nap with. The bottom-floor simply won't work, as there will be too much noise, or people wandering in occasionally to borrow a glass of water.

If it is hot at this particular beach, as most are, turn the air conditioning as low as it will go before lying down to snooze. Little-known fact: Hotels and condominiums do not charge extra for power usage. Turn down the AC, let the refrigerator door stay open for hours, leave the hair dryer on – it doesn't matter.

For a home nap, I usually don't have the luxury of much solitude, making the fundamentals for a perfect nap slightly different.

The prelude is basically the same – active morning outdoors, preferably a golf outing, followed by a hearty meal. Retirement is usually to my bedroom. I am a "sleep on top of the covers" napper, so I make sure the bed is made. Just my personal preference.

I turn the TV on to something like a baseball game or Formula One racing or women's college basketball – something in which I can't get too interested. The sound is barely audible. The AC is set for 68-70 (unfortunately, the hotel won't pay my power bill – despite my pleadings), and a ceiling fan is going full-blast. A UGA afghan rests nearby in case a chill emerges. I place a dark baseball cap on my head with the bill directly over my eyes. The Land of Nod soon beckons, and it is glorious.

Do yourself a favor: Take a nap today. If you can't seem to fall asleep, read this column three more times.

Diary of a swing through the South
July 20, 2005

The numbers are as follows: 1,828 miles driven; 35 hours driving; $181.96 spent on gasoline; $101.37 spent on diet colas, coffee, Blow-Pops, and Cheez-Its; 14 viewings of "Shrek 2" on the DVD player; 14 minutes – the lifespan of headphones bought for the DVD player before being destroyed by my three-year-old son; 1 priceless vase broken when it was stepped on in an effort to retrieve "Shrek 2" for another viewing; 1,828 pieces of crumbled Cheez-Its picked up off the van floor.

Those are the raw statistics from my family's recent journey from Homerville, Georgia, to Ft. Smith, Arkansas, and back. But as Mark Twain so squarely put it: "There are lies, darn lies (edited for family newspapers), and statistics." That data only tells part of the story of our swing across the Southern states to visit kinfolks. The rest can be rightly surmised from the brief diary I kept of our land-laden voyage. It is as follows:

Tuesday, 2:15 p.m. – Leave Homerville. We're not out of the city when my six-year-old daughter starts whimpering.

"What's wrong, honey?" My wife asks.

"I miss Yo-Yo. I'm afraid something's going to happen to him," she sobs.

I reassure her that our cat has plenty of food and water and will be fine.

Tuesday, 6:30 p.m. – We stop in Montgomery, Alabama to get a bite, go to the restroom, and let the kids run around a little. Twelve minutes after getting back on the road, we have to stop to go to the bathroom again. Ditto, 35 minutes later. Our five hours in Alabama is littered with such stops, leading me to the conclusion that Alabama has the dirtiest convenience store bathrooms in the continental United States.

Wednesday, 12:30 a.m. – We stop in Tupelo, Mississippi, to spend the night. Unfortunately, Elvis' birthplace isn't open after midnight.

Wednesday, 9 a.m. – We're on the road again. My daughter keeps wanting to stop to buy Yo-Yo "a present." I ignore her request.

Wednesday, 2:30 p.m. – Of all the states I've been to, Arkansas clearly has the best names for towns. We just went through Possum Grape and Bald Knob, and saw signs for Toad Suck and Oil Trough.

That almost makes up for the sad fact that they don't serve their tea sweet.

Wednesday, 7:45 p.m. – We make it to Fort Smith, which is on the Arkansas-Oklahoma border. A spatula and a crowbar are utilized to pry the underside of my legs from the leather driver's seat.

Wednesday, 10:30 p.m.-Friday, 9:30 a.m. – No diary entries are made, because I am sleeping.

Friday, 12:15 p.m. – We make another journey – this one of two hours – to Eureka Springs, Arkansas. Eureka Springs is called "Arkansas's Little Switzerland" – sort of an Alpine village built on the side of a mountain. The winding downtown area is full of antique and collectible shops and art galleries. I put a 10-gallon bucket around my wife's neck to control the salivating.

Friday, 4:30 p.m. – We're pooped. My wife, though, has a crazed look in her eye. She grabs the only member of our crew who isn't zombiatic (a word I just made up) and disappears for an hour. Later, her unwitting sidekick – our three-year-old son – walks up to an antique trunk in a store and asks the clerk, "What's this? A treasure chest?"

"Sort of," the woman replied.

He then asked: "Is there a dead guy in it?"

She thought that hilarious. Of course, most any quip is comical when coming from under a red felt firemen's helmet.

Saturday, 7 p.m. – We start our return home.

Saturday, 11:32 p.m. – I'm scanning the radio when I hear "In the Navy" by the Village People. I haven't heard that song in at least 25 years. I wonder aloud why the U.S. Navy doesn't use that song in their recruiting ads. Nobody hears me because I'm the only one awake.

Sunday, 2:10 a.m. – We spend the night at a hotel in New Albany, Mississippi. Once we get into the room, my one-year-old son decides it's time to play. I fall asleep at 3:35 a.m.

Sunday, 4:45 a.m. – In Alabama again. My wife keeps asking me about how we should decorate our daughter's bedroom. I'm nodding in agreement to everything she says, but I'm really thinking about the best cheeseburgers I've ever had.

Sunday, 8:45 p.m. – We finally get home.

The second I open our back door, I hear Yo-Yo, the cat, crying from the back of the house. I open our bedroom door to find that we have locked him in there for five days.

Add another number to our journey: 16 – the number of presents Yo-Yo left on our bed.

The Remedial Guide to Bringing Up Baby
August 3, 2005

Over the next month, both my sister and sister-in-law will be having their first respective children, and I can't wait to find out if I'm an aunt or an uncle.

I'm looking forward to years of teaching my nephews and/or nieces the same kinds of valuable life lessons I was taught by my uncles: Obscene hand gestures; that hilarious pull-my-finger trick; how to make funny flatulent noises with my armpit; a songbook of limericks that start with "there once was a man from Nantucket..."

I was a very popular person in eighth grade thanks to the positive influence of my cadre of uncles.

But this column isn't about me and my juvenile record. It's about how young future parents like my sister and her husband and sister-in-law and her husband can be better prepared parents. I've been through that wringer – three times already – and have some sage advice/insight/warnings that all expecting parents should know and commit to memory. Following is my remedial guide for such first-time parents dealing with babies. Read it, know it, live it.

Prepare to be knowledgeable:

• First, there's a soft spot on the top of the baby's head. Although it may look like a button, it's not. You are not to press it.

• The first four months of a baby's life are not fun for the parents. Basically, your goal as a parent should be to keep the child alive. After the fourth month, the baby starts acting and looking more like a human being and it starts to be enjoyable.

• Fathers – treat an infant just as you would a can of Coke. If you shake it up a little, it's going to spew all over you – usually when you're wearing a suit.

• A normal temperature for a human being is 98.6 degrees. There is no need to rush your baby to the emergency room when its temperature reaches 99 degrees.

• At some point, your baby will be dropped on the floor.

The child may simply fall out of your arms, or roll off a couch or bed. Make sure you're not the first parent to do it.

• For a while after the baby is born, all kinds of people are going to come to your house to "see the baby." Why? I don't know. They aren't coming to see you, so I suggest you use that free time to take a nap. Trust me – you'll need it.

• Fathers – the mother of your child may show signs of psychosis (from what I've heard, of course) after the baby is born. Don't worry – this wears off after a decade or so.

• If you hold any pretenses that you'll still be "cool" after your first child is born – forget it.

You are now a parent. Go ahead and pull your pants up real high, cancel your subscription to *Rolling Stone,* and purchase a mini-van. It's over. You'll never be cool again.

• On the other hand, you will be up a lot at 3:30 a.m., and it's a little-known fact that MTV still plays music videos when nobody is supposed to be watching. So you may get to catch up on the latest, hippest hits. At 3:30, the only other non-infomercial programming are repeats of "Gomer Pyle USMC," which I highly recommend.

• On that note, when the baby wakes you up in the middle of the night crying – loud, fake snoring will work for about two-to-three months until your spouse figures it out.

• Mothers – the father of your child may try to avoid certain parenting duties like changing diapers or feeding the baby or staying in the same room as the child. Don't permit that. Let them share in the parenting duties – not necessarily to give you a break, but rather because if they aren't allowed or expected to be a participating parent, they won't be. And they will be missing out on so, so much.

Like I said – sage advice.

Mission statements need diverse synergy
August 24, 2005

A number of years ago, in a futile attempt to appear like a visionary leader, I wasted about 30 seconds of my life coming up with our newspaper's goals. I then printed out these goals and taped them to walls around the office.

They said:

"Our goals are:

1. Serve our customers.

2. Get it right.

3. Make money.

4.-10. Serve our customers."

I failed to print our goals 11.-20. – Avoid being sued.

That's about the closest I have come to crafting a mission statement.

I bring up mission statements because I spoke with a friend of mine recently who works in an office where everyone has titles that don't mean anything – I think he's a Regional Quality Consultant, or perhaps a Product Accounts Associate – I can't remember. Anyway, he told me that he went on a corporate retreat where a bunch of people from his office spent the entire day in a hotel conference room coming up with a mission statement for their company. An entire day! Not one of my entire work days either – which is something like four-to-five hours including a nap – but one of those hellish eight-hour work days where you can't go home to go to the bathroom.

"So what did ya'll come up with? It must be a doozy," I told him, thinking eight hours should create an epic manifesto that starts with Adam and Eve, goes through Burt Reynolds' work in the "Smokey and the Bandit" movies, and ends with the Red Sox winning the World Series.

He couldn't remember what it said, then scoured through some papers and dictated this, their mission statement: "Our company's mission is to strive to synergistically foster a diverse atmosphere in an effort to professionally enhance mission-critical data to stay competitive in our market and better serve our customers."

That took eight hours? I was baffled. "Okay, what does that mean?"

"I don't know," he admitted.

Not having to spend eight hours crafting a mission statement, I did some research on these time-drenching declarations of mission, and why every business, organization, and entity known to mankind is spending their respective energy to have one.

Here's what I found:

First, mission statements must include at least two of the following phrases, words, or derivations thereof to be considered an acceptable mission statement: Synergy, empowerment, high-performance, diversity, professional, and/or competitive.

Also, using language that isn't incredibly ambiguous is apparently a breach of mission-statement etiquette, as is the inclusion of proper nouns.

Secondly, there is much confusion about the difference between a mission statement and a vision statement. Think of it this way: A mission statement is to a vision statement as ketchup is to catsup.

According to the experts who actually get paid to write mission statements for folks with entirely too much money, mission statements are absolutely critical to a business or organization. Without a mission, they say in vague verbiage, how can an employee know what to do?

For instance, let's say my friend, the Regional Quality Systems Product Accounts Associate Consultant, has a customer that asks him to do something unethical. What should he do? Consult the mission statement, of course.

Hmm, "... to strive to synergistically foster a diverse atmosphere in an effort to professionally enhance mission-critical data..."

Uh, never mind.

After my 34-minute probe into mission statements, I'm sold. Boy, how did I ever live without one?

I decided to craft my own mission statement. It took 12 seconds to make up and I didn't have to rent a hotel conference room to concoct it. My mission statement is: Stay out of jail.

I have printed copies of my mission statement to post around our house.

I hope they don't end up in the same place as my "newspaper goals" I posted around the office – in the garbage can.

Three-year-old boy + restroom = Danger!
September 7, 2005

My mother warned me about wearing clean underwear in case I was in an automobile accident. My father warned me about dating women with tattoos. And my grandmother warned me about "staying away from that doping mess."

All were heeded.

But in all my 30-something years of life, all 12 years of public school education, all seven years of college, nobody, not one soul, ever warned me about the inherent pitfalls, humiliations, and physical dangers involved with taking a three-year-old boy to the toilet.

Perhaps some of you who have had a three-year-old boy know what I'm talking about. And I'm not talking about a three-year-old boy going to the bathroom at home. At home, you just send him in there by his lonesome and hope someone else discovers the carnage.

No, I'm talking about public restrooms – bathrooms at restaurants or movie theaters or churches or ballgames, where the father is the person that has to escort the son to go "tee-tee."

I'll give you a recent example of what this involves.

First, three-year-old boys don't understand the unwritten canons of conduct in men's restrooms. This code dictates that you don't start up conversations in the bathroom. You avoid eye-contact and if you happen to accidentally make eye-contact, a friendly nod with a silent "hey" is as much as etiquette allows. Only when you're at a ballgame are you allowed to break protocol and speak semi-freely, and then only if you are talking about the athletic contest at hand.

Three-year-old boys don't understand this concept yet. I think it kicks in when they turn 10.

Even though I've tried to explain this to him, when my three-year-old son enters a public restroom, he talks to everyone, and about everyone, he sees.

Back to my example. So, this weekend, we walk into a men's restroom at a restaurant. My son spots a small urinal. "Look, it's kid sized!" He quickly darts to the urinal and begins his flawed technique.

Grown men usually don't drop their pants all the way to the floor when they're going to the bathroom. As they have discovered through years of trial-and-error, bathroom floors are often wet where other men have missed the target. But three-year-old boys don't have years of this experience, and won't listen to their fathers when they try to explain the flaws of such an action.

So he drops his pants completely to the floor before I can stop them.

At this point, a very large man, apparently a biker, walks into the bathroom. I have my hand on my son's soggy shorts as he does his business. The man is wearing a bandanna on his head, with huge tattoos shining off his bulging biceps. As this behemoth steers toward a stall, my son looks over his shoulder at him and screams, "Hey, Daddy – look, it's a pirate!"

I suddenly had to urinate too.

Luckily, the man apparently didn't hear the pirate remark or perhaps didn't feel like bludgeoning anyone at that moment. But my son, being the restroom conversationalist, persisted.

"Hey, Mr. Pirate, are you going to tee..." At this point, his line of questioning was muffled by my hand which wasn't holding up his pants. In between my fingers, he kept on chattering.

We quickly pulled up his pants and headed toward the sink to wash his hands. Of course, the sink is not built for three-year-olds, so I have to lift him up with one hand while I squirt liquid soap into his hands. This frees his mouth to continue the dialogue with Mr. Pirate.

"Daddy, do you think Mr. Pirate knows Spiderman, or Mr. Krabs, or..."

The hand-washing process took all of 4.5 seconds. I carried him out of the restroom like a sack of potatoes, trying to hit the exit before Mr. Pirate got out of the stall.

We made it this time. But he doesn't turn 10 for another seven years.

Let this serve as the warning I never received.

And they call us lazy Americans
September 21, 2005

About a year and a half ago in this space, I mused about how I needed to accomplish a world record to give some meaning – or something demeaning – to my life.

Since most world records require effort, I pondered creating my own category – "layting" – laying down while eating.

Dang if they don't actually have a world record for that already.

This from an *Associated Press* wire story: Recently, Suresh Joachim broke the Guinness World Record for the longest time spent watching television – commonly known as the "couch potato" record. He finished at 69 hours, 48 minutes; breaking the previous record of 50 hours, seven minutes.

According to the story, "rules for the couch potato honor, as stipulated by Guinness, allow for a five-minute break every hour and a 15-minute break every eight hours. The viewer must otherwise be constantly looking at the screen."

The story also notes that this is Joachim's 16th world record. His other record-breaking feats include the longest duration balancing on one foot (over 76 hours) and for marathon bowling (100 hours). Joachim, who lives in Toronto, Canada, but hails from Sri Lanka, said he attempts to break world records "to raise awareness of suffering children."

In the story, it states that Suresh watched only ABC shows during his record-breaking lounge. Yes, that indeed does raise awareness about suffering children – and adults for that matter.

I have a couple of comments to impart about Suresh (which, translated from Sinhalese, is English for "Dewayne") and his record.

First, the criteria for this record seems rather weak. A five-minute break every hour and a 15-minute break every eight hours? That's for sissies.

Heck, back in 1994, I sat on my couch and watched TV for 28 straight hours without any type of break. It was Labor Day weekend and my air conditioner was broke. I sat a cooler and two large bags of Doritos next to the couch and watched the entire 24-hour "Andy Griffith Show" marathon, then four hours of "Law & Order" (there's an episode on at least one channel at all times) before falling asleep.

I didn't need a bathroom break because I sweat out every liquid in my body. If I had just known I only needed 22 more hours to break a world record, I would have watched the uncut version of "Once Upon A Time in America" a couple of times.

Secondly, having a Sri Lankan/Canadian hold the world's "couch potato" record is akin to a team of Russians winning baseball's World Series. As a country, we should be embarrassed.

For years, we have enjoyed a worldwide reputation as "lazy Americans." What has happened to us? Where is our pride? Where's our "can't-do" spirit? Certainly we have Americans lazier that this Suresh fellow. We are too lazy to roll up our car windows or manually brush our teeth, but we're not lazy enough to lay on a couch for 50 hours? Shame on us! C'mon, America, get off your bum and be lethargic!

Next time they broadcast that "Andy Griffith Show" marathon, I'm on the couch, bags and bags of processed potato-like products in tow, representing the greatest land of loafers there ever was – the gosh-darn United States of America!

This record calls for an American who is equal parts shiftless, lazy, and slothful – and I think I'm just the man to do it. Unless, of course, I can't find any batteries for my remote control. Then someone else will have to do it.

Heredity rears its jabbering head
October 12, 2005

When I was in third grade, my desk was placed outside the classroom – in the hall. This was done, my teacher said, as a preventive measure to ensure the other kids had a chance to learn something.

"You talk so much, Len, that these other children can't get an education when you're in there," she told me.

She failed to mention how my education was improved by sitting at a desk in an empty hall with no pencil, paper, books or instruction. Occasionally, they would allow me back in the classroom for birthday parties or tornado drills or when they wanted the erasers cleaned. I would contain myself for about 40 seconds before bursting into what Mr. T would derisively categorize as "jibber-jabber," and then I would be exiled again to my hall.

I learned to control my loquaciousness in subsequent years, and was actually allowed in the classroom for most of high school.

I have no idea how many times my wife was placed outside of her classroom during her school days, but I imagine it was often. As an adult, she basically vocalizes every one of her thought processes, so I'm going to assume that she was at least just as talkative as a child.

That said, it is no wonder that our daughter, who is in first grade, has sometimes found herself in the dreaded "warning box."

Every day after school, before we can even ask, our daughter tells us what "box" she was in that school day. There are apparently three boxes in elementary school. There is the "happy box." From what I've heard from my daughter, this box is reserved for children who are well-behaved. Then there is the aforementioned "warning box." Children who act up slightly are placed in this box. It is, as its name implies, a warning that should you misbehave any more, you will be placed in the next level of boxes. The third and most feared box is known as the "sad box." The "sad box," legend has it, is where the stallions of elementary school horseplay reside; prepubescent purgatory if you will.

I don't know what these boxes look like, if they are cardboard or wood, or how big or small they are. I do know that the happy box is apparently filled with candy. I would imagine that the warning box is full of, I don't know, warnings, and that the sad box is rife with razors, upside-down tacks, and shards of glass.

But, inevitably, if our daughter is not in the happy box, the reason for such is the same: Talking. She just likes to talk a lot.

I had high hopes that genetics wouldn't be so cruel to our son. But as he reaches the midway point of his third year, I believe his gabby ancestry has taken hold.

Lately, he begins and ends all his garbled diatribes the same.

"When I was a baby," starts his whimsical rant. "... And then the tiger fell in the water" ends it. An abbreviated example: "When I was a baby, I went to Wild Adventures, and we saw a dinosaur, and he ate a doggy, and I saw his snomach, and it had a snake in it, and then the tiger fell in the water."

"Son, we went to Wild Adventures yesterday," I respond.

Not understanding the concept of time, or brevity, he chats away.

"When I was a baby, the doctor found an octopus in my pajamas...," and it goes on and on and on until the tiger falls in the water.

And we have another child, who at one, has yet to break into song. I'm sure he's saving up for later.

Teachers, go ahead and place the desks outside the classroom. I'm sorry, but I'm afraid they're coming your way.

'Twas the night of our sickness...
November 16, 2005

The players: Myself, my wife, my six-year-old daughter, three-year-old son, one-year-old son, a king-size bed, a queen-size bed, two twin beds, three bedrooms, a couch, a wiener dog named Bubby, and a virus. We'll call it Mr. Vomit.

The scene: A regular, ordinary Tuesday night in our home.

7:52 p.m.: Our youngest son goes to sleep in his twin bed.

8:39 p.m.: Our two other children go to bed – our daughter in her queen bed; our three-year-old son in his twin bed in the bedroom he shares with his brother.

11:01 p.m.: My wife and I lie down for nod in our king-size bed.

11:03 p.m.: My wife is awakened by the sound of loud hacking coming from our sons' bedroom. Upon inspection, she finds that our youngest son has coughed up his dinner, his lunch, and four of the tiny soaps that used to be in the bathroom.

My wife cleans him up, changes the sheets, and then lies down next to him to calm him down. After a while, they both fall asleep in his bed.

12:09 a.m.: Our daughter, as is her custom, sneaks out of her room and stealthily slithers under our bed's sheets.

1:19 a.m.: Our youngest son has another vomiting episode, this time throwing up on himself, my wife and all over his bed. They change clothes and both squeeze into our king bed.

1:52 a.m.: My wife is awakened by the cries of our three-year-old son. She finds him sitting upright in his bed with a perfect circle of vomit in the epicenter of his bed. She scoops him up and brings him to our bed, where now five humans have accumulated.

2:13 a.m.: As is my custom, I awaken in the middle of the night with a child's foot in my ear. Oblivious to the previous events, I pick up our three-year-old son, carry him to his bed and plop him down – right in the middle of his puddle of puke.

I trudge to the bathroom, where I clean him up, then we head to his sister's empty, barf-less bed.

3:41 a.m.: Our youngest son wakes up and coughs up another stream, miring half of our bed in stench. A quick check of the remaining sleeping areas finds them either soaked with spew or occupied.

My wife considers changing sheets again, but she's too exhausted. She leaves our sleeping daughter on the clean side of our bed and heads to the couch in the living room, where she, our youngest son, and Bubby the wiener dog cuddle up to snooze.

4:14 a.m.: Our youngest son strikes again, hitting the couch and its environs. Bubby quickly begins feasting on my son's retched refuse, which, as is her custom, prompted my wife to hurl. Bubby found that appetizing as well, which produced even more gagging.

After locking Bubby out of the house, perhaps with a drop-kick, my wife goes back to our bedroom, where she looks and looks for clean fitted sheets. She can't find any, so she wakes up our daughter, takes off the half-clean sheet and puts a series of twin sheets on the bed. Then she, our daughter, and our youngest son go to sleep there.

5:29 a.m.: I awake to find my son's mug about half an inch from my face.

"Daddy, is the world a ball?"

His breath smelled of Cheez-Its and bile.

"Huh?"

"Daddy, I threw up again," he said matter-of-factly. I looked down. Between us oozed a river of regurgitation.

We got out of bed, surveyed the available accommodations, and determined that squeezing in the muddled king-size bed was our best bet.

6:05 a.m.: Sun comes up, and with it, as is their custom, both of our sons.

I awake to find my three-year-old son's face about half an inch from my face, his brother gleefully bouncing on the edge of our bed.

"Daddy, where does the moon go during the day?"

"To sleep," I groaned.

It wasn't over. That night: Same story, different players, as is Mr. Vomit's custom.

Offering a prayer for the prey
December 28, 2005

I was basking in the post-Christmas light on my porch while the children frolicked in the backyard. At my hand was a sterling glass of sweet tea. At my foot, a menagerie of mismatched wrenches, screwdrivers, scissors and C batteries. I was wondering why the packaging for the Fisher-Price Little People Musical Christmas Train was more secure than the Pentagon when tragedy struck.

The screams came from the corner of the yard, where our six-year-old daughter and four-year-old son had been digging holes in the dirt for reasons that escape me, or them.

"Daddy! Daddy! Daddy!," they bellowed in unison, frantically running toward me with arms waving wildly. "Emergency! Emergency! Emergency!," yelled my daughter. "Daddy, it's an emergency! Call the paraplegics!"

It was an emergency, so I let it go.

"What? What?," I replied, rising leisurely to my feet. "What's wrong?"

"It's Yo-Yo, Daddy!," my daughter huffed, referring to the family feline. "He's killed something! Come help!"

They then grabbed my hands and dragged me to the corner of the yard, where Yo-Yo was having dinner over what appeared to be a squirrel.

"Daddy, see!," she said, pointing to our cat and his entree. "Do something!"

I delayed action, which prompted my daughter to take matters in her own little hands. As she reached out to grab Yo-Yo, I reached out and grabbed her.

"No, no, no," I said calmly. "You don't mess with an animal while they are eating. They'll bite you. See, that's nature. Yo-Yo hunted down that squirrel and pounced on it. That's what cats, and other animals, do. They eat animals smaller than them. That's how they survive."

We then had a dialogue about the laws of nature and the food chain – me explaining to them something I know nothing about, and them listening with concerned, puzzled brows. Somewhere, a science teacher fainted.

When I was done with my nonsensical monologue, my daughter, the animal lover, said, "Daddy, I want to say a prayer for the squirrel."

"Okay, go ahead," I said through my grin.

She cleared her throat and we bowed our heads.

"Lord, please be with this squirrel, and let him have his legs, stomach, head, and neck back when he gets to Heaven," she said. "And Lord, please be with all the other squirrels and small animals and don't let them be eaten by larger animals." She lifted her head for a second, then down again. "Oh, and Lord, please forgive Yo-Yo. I guess he was hungry. Let us buy more cat food not made of squirrel for him to eat. Amen."

We raised our heads and then my son, who had been just a confused observer up to this point, chimed in. "I want to say a prayer too. Me too! Me too!"

"Okay, son, go ahead," I said.

He cleared his throat, hesitated, then offered: "God is great, God is good, let us thank Him for our food. By His hands we are fed. Thank you Lord for our daily bread. Amen."

About then, their mother called from the house. Lunch was almost ready, she announced. Knowing their mother hated to see dead animals, they quickly hatched a plan. My son got his mittens and picked up what was left of the squirrel – just his tail – and they then buried it in one of their backyard holes. "Mommy will never find it there," he reasoned.

We then saddled up to the table for lunch, where hearty helpings of ham were being served.

They didn't ask where ham came from, and I wasn't about to tell them.

Did I forget to write this column?
March 15, 2006

The answering machine message light signified a blinking "5."

Five messages! Five people who want to talk to me! Who could it be? Maybe I've won something! It could be an old friend calling to catch up. That would be nice. Or maybe those calls are for my wife. That's more likely. Or my daughter. Or my sons. It's probably that doggedly-persistent college loan guy. It could be five people with the wrong number. Maybe it's some crank calls. People just don't make crank calls like they used to. I remember back when I was a kid, we used to make crank calls all the time...

Two hours later, I walked into my bedroom and saw the answering machine light blinking "5." Hmm, I wonder who's calling? This time, my mind didn't wander aimlessly. Instead, I walked up and pressed the play button.

The first message was from my wife, apparently to herself: "Hello, remember you have to sign your son up for Pre-K today." The second message was from my wife, to herself: "Hey, don't forget that those reports are due by Thursday." The third message was from my wife, to herself, I hope: "Remember to get the scrapbooking stuff out of the attic and arrange the new pictures." The fourth message was from my wife, to, yes, herself: "Hey, it's me. Don't forget to pick up your dress from the cleaners by Friday." And the fifth message was from my wife, to herself, with a twist: "Hey, I almost forgot that I need to get that gift for the party, which is Saturday at 3 p.m. And also take a dessert. That's it. Love you, bye."

My wife leaves such messages on our answering machine so she won't forget something – or forget that she loves herself.

It's an issue that seems to confront all two of the adults in our household. Being an old-school scribe, I opt for the written word – penning notes to myself whenever the urge or athazagoraphobia (fear of forgetting) hits. Unfortunately, the only time I seem to be of clear mind where I can remember my appointments or commitments is when I'm in bed, in the dark, right before my entrance into the Land of Nod. Thus, my bedside scribblings often look like: "Meetings with ZZy7rens at 14 p.m. rember to bring cloak." In the morning, or three days later, that's not very helpful.

Our mental malaise can't yet be explained by senility. We're too junior to have "senior moments." But more and more, my wife and I seem feeble of mind and memory. Where we used to finish each others' sentences, we now can't even finish a sentence.

It can be quite embarrassing in a social setting, as I found out recently.

"So Bill Clinton, George Bush, the Pope, and a parakeet walk into a bar. Before they sit down, they... uh... well... why is everyone looking at me?"

"You were telling a joke, Len."

"I was?," I stammered, not being able to recall what I was talking about, or who these people standing around me were. "Well, it wasn't very funny anyway. Carry on."

According to my notes, I have chalked up this mental infirmity to having three young children, and the scientific fact that having children makes parents stupider. Or maybe it's having parents makes children stupider. I can't recall exactly, but you can look it up on the computer thingy where they have words and such.

The point is: I believe this is a temporary state; that our lapses of memory will become more infrequent over time, then, of course, more frequent over time, until one day, I will consistently call my children by the wrong names, which only happens inconsistently now. Either way, I'm not a complete idiot yet. I may be forgetful, and absent-minded, and unaware, and forgetful, and a complete idiot, but I'm no communist.

Let me write that down before I forget it.

What boy doesn't want a pet monkey?

It's hard to tell your children no – except when they ask for a pet monkey.

"Daddy, can I get a monkey?"

"No," I answered my four-year-old son without even looking up from my newspaper.

"Why not?"

"Well, for one, you already have a little brother," I replied, again, not looking up from the sports page. "He's sort of like a monkey."

"But Daddy, I need a monkey to do things for me," he reasoned. "You know what? He can help me clean my room. He can play with me and jump on the ceiling. I'll play music and he'll jump up and down. You know what? I can have him fight the dog and you can watch it too. And he'll only eat a little bit of gum and straw. And, you know what? He can also help you do... whatever you do. I'll take care of him myself."

I put my paper down to quash this monkey business.

"Look, son, having a pet monkey seems like a lot of fun, but it's not all it's made up to be," I said, looking into his sad face. "Monkeys don't do what you say. They won't do tricks unless paid cash. They are difficult to toilet-train. They often become chain smokers. And once they've been pets, no lab will even considering buying them. Every boy dreams of having his own pet monkey – I did too. But they simply aren't good pets."

This quieted him up for a bit. He returned with a fresh desire.

"Daddy, can I get a wizard?"

"A wizard? What are you talking about?"

"You know, a wizard," he replied.

"Huh? You mean an old man that dresses in a shiny gown and does tricks?"

"Nooo," he said, giggling. "I'm talking about a wizard. You know, he's gween and cwawls on the gwound and eat bugs – a wizard."

I got it.

"You mean, a lizard, with an L," I said, accentuating the "L."

"Yes, sir, that's what I said – a wizard," he replied.

"Sure, go find one," I said, going back to my paper. He scurried away and I didn't see him for an hour.

Later, he limped into the room as I was dozing off.

"Daddy, I couldn't find a wizard," he moaned.

"Sorry to hear that," I muttered.

"Daddy, you know what?"

"What?"

"Daddy, can I have an earring?"

This startled me from my near-nap.

"An earring?!! You're a four-year-old boy. Why do you want an earring?"

"I saw a pirate with one on TV," he answered to my hysteria.

"A pirate on TV? Well, if a pirate on TV was jumping off a cliff, would you jump off too?"

"Pirates don't jump off cliffs, Daddy. They jump off pwanks," he said in a semi-scoffing manner.

"Okay, if a pirate was jumping off a plank, would you jump too?"

"Yes, sir. That would be great!"

I laid back down.

"Daddy, can I get an earring?"

"No."

"Daddy, can I get a pirate then? He can help me clean my room. And you know what? We can play with swords and we won't tear up the curtains. And you know..."

"Aaargh!"

Do we cheat them? And how!

May 3, 2006

According to the 49 e-mails I receive a day from residents of the continent of Africa, there are large sums of money sitting in banks there unclaimed.

If the people of this continent just have cash lying around, and I just had to pay $56 to fill up my car's gas tank here in the U.S. of A., I figure it's worth a shot to send a message to one of its residents in an effort to help pay my gas bill, and buy a fishing boat or two.

As you will probably notice, I have written this letter in their brand of English to secure their confidence.

Attn: Request for Partnership
Dear Sir/Madam:

Compliments of the day and my best wishes to you. I wish to introduce myself. I am Len Robbins, Executive Governor of the Bank of the United States of America – Homerville, Georgia branch.

The issue at hand is in respect to a sum of money, $27, 500,000.00 US dollars already in our correspondent private banking. Originated by my predecessor, he could not complete the transfer as he was killed in the civil war by the rebels from, oh, let's say, South Dakota.

However, while going through all the transfers made upon my appointment, I happened to run into this transfer still virgin.

This account was opened by a foreigner. Upon maturity, I sent a routine notification to his forwarding address but received no reply. Finally we discovered the foreigner had died in a hotdog eating contest accident (very common here). On further investigation, I found that he died without making a Will, and all attempts to contact next of kin were abortive as no one has come to claim his funds. According to the laws of my country, after 5 (five) months, the funds will be unclaimed and revert to oil company profits.

In order to avert this development, I now seek your permission to allow an attorney (from the much respected lawyer firm of Dewey, Cheatham & Howe) to do a backdated Will in your name, so the funds can be released to you as the beneficiary of the fund so that I will use my vital power and personality to back you up so that we can join hand together to obtain the necessary document that will back the fund and make sure that the money is transferred into your account.

Hence, I solicit your indulgence to assist and see that the total sum of money is transferred to your bank account and to be shared at the ratio of 50% 50% each.

I will not fail to bring to your notice that this business transaction is 100% risk and trouble free and that you should not entertain any fear as all modalities for fund transfer can be finalized within 7 to 9 banking days. You are only required to send me your full name, banking account number for the transfer, age and marital status, and amount currently in your banking account, and $80,000.00 US dollars to pay fees for much respected lawyer firm of Dewey, Cheatham & Howe.

Please note that this transaction is strictly confidential and must be treated with utmost secrecy. When you send the funds to the much respected lawyer firm Dewey, Cheatham & Howe, I will explain how I came about your coordinates.

Yours faithfully,
Executive Governor
Len Robbins

As they say in Ghana, what's good for the gander is good for the geeses.

Adventures in 'child-proofing'

May 24, 2006

Prior to the birth of our first child seven years ago, my wife went bananas "child-proofing" our house.

She put locks and latches on every cabinet. She put coverings on every outlet. She cut every window blind cord. She installed carbon monoxide and smoke detectors in every room of the house. She threw away every concert t-shirt I had.

She never fully explained how that last one made our home safer for a child.

Anyway, months later, I appreciated the wisdom of her efforts, as our curious daughter quickly scooted from room to room seeking danger, only to find little.

Two more children, the youngest now two, and I have realized that "child-proofing" is an inappropriate term. What my wife did should be called "baby-proofing." I say that because we now have three children and our home, despite our best efforts, is not "child-proof." Not even close. And I don't think it's ever going to be.

Here is what we would have to do to make our home truly "child-proof."

1. Eliminate all water.

To our children, water is a magical, mystical plaything – something to be thrown about, tossed in the air, tickled, and poured on hardwood floors to create a hallway slip-n-slide.

They have mastered the art of turning on faucets, yet haven't figured how to turn them off, which is quite problematic.

We have found that water, when combined with seemingly innocuous items, equates big messes. For instance, the other day I saw a bucket full of toys in the play room and thought nothing of it. Fifteen minutes later, our two-year-old son, using his advanced faucet-turning skills, had filled the aforementioned bucket full of water and was chasing the cat down the hall.

2. Eliminate all paper products.

Of particular nuisance is toilet paper.

Newly-minted to the joys of "pottying," our sons in particular have an affinity for creative uses of toilet paper. We'll find rolls all over the house – some they have scribbled on, others that have torn into tiny little bits, they rolled their older sister's room yesterday. But more often, actually daily, we'll find one or two rolls just sitting in the toilet – soaked and useless. And that stuff doesn't grow on trees.

3. Eliminate all food products.

Actually, we wouldn't need to eliminate all food products. They won't mess with a pineapple, for instance. But nearly all other foods in our home have found themselves used in some type of non-edible fashion by our children.

For example, I found a half-eaten banana in the VCR yesterday... and a half-eaten granola bar in one of my church shoes... and what used to be a half-eaten popsicle on Page 42 of "Letters from a Nut."

Perhaps if we just starved them, they would finish what they started eating and we wouldn't have this problem. (Note to self: Start starving children.)

Unfortunately, after consulting a statistician, we have come to the conclusion that we are outnumbered (3-to-2). Instead of chasing them with a mop around the house, we must get them to modify their behavior – particularly that little, curious one that's always up to no good. Or, as the statistician suggested, we could eliminate all the water, paper and food in the house. That would sufficiently "child-proof" it.

As long as we keep cable, I'm fine with that.